Maps, Charts, Graphs, and Diagrams

Skill Building Activities for Visual Literacy (Intermediate)

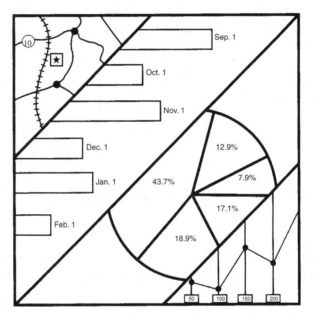

Written by John and Patty Carratello

Illustrated by Paula Spence and Keith Vasconcelles

Teacher Created Materials, Inc.
6421 Industry Way
Westminster, CA 92683
www.teachercreated.com
©1990 Teacher Created Materials, Inc.
Reprinted, 2003
Made in U.S.A.
ISBN-1-55734-169-9

Table of Contents

Introduction

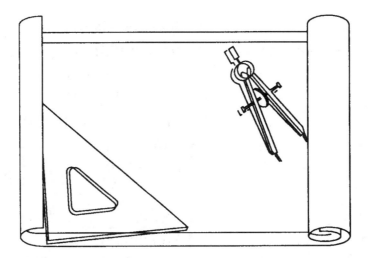

Maps, Charts, Graphs, and Diagrams

Words aren't always the best way to communicate information. For this reason, we often use pictures— maps, charts, graphs, and diagrams—to help us. The old saying that "a picture can equal a thousand words" is so very true.

With this book, teachers can give students many hands-on opportunities to practice using these visual tools in a meaningful context. Students will learn how to read different types of maps, charts, graphs, and diagrams, as well as how to construct their own. They will also learn which visual tools are best for presenting specific types of information. Work may be completed independently, in a group, or as a class.

The activities have been designed to help teachers introduce, teach, or reinforce the concepts of maps, charts, graphs, and diagrams. However, some students may require a more basic introduction to these skills. **Beginning Maps** *and* **Beginning Charts, Graphs, and Diagrams,** *two other books in this series, can provide such an introduction.*

We hope these pages will help you guide your students toward visual literacy.

Maps, Charts, Graphs, and Diagrams

Maps, charts, graphs, and *diagrams* are visual tools. They give us a way to see information easily. It is sometimes easier to see information in a map, chart, graph, or diagram than it is to hear it or read it.

Study these examples of a map, chart, graph, and diagram.

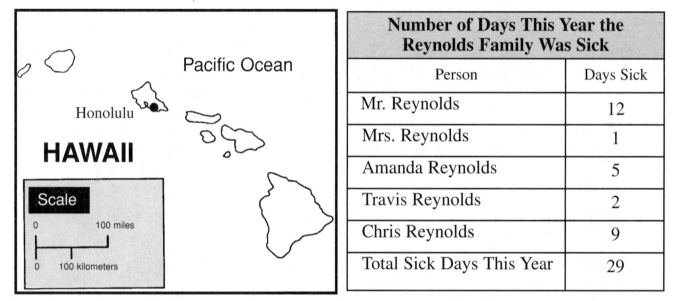

Map

Number of Days This Year the Reynolds Family Was Sick	
Person	Days Sick
Mr. Reynolds	12
Mrs. Reynolds	1
Amanda Reynolds	5
Travis Reynolds	2
Chris Reynolds	9
Total Sick Days This Year	29

Chart

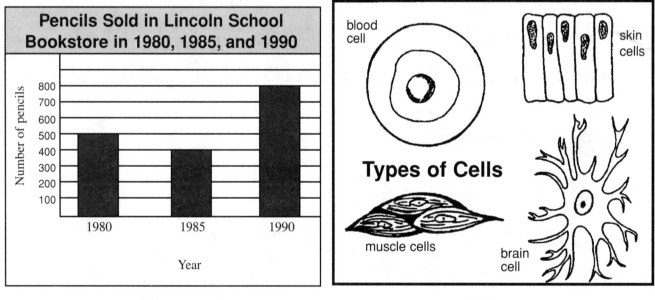

GRAPH

DIAGRAM

*Find an example of a map, chart, graph, and diagram to share with your class.

What Is a Map?

A map is a picture of a place. A map may give general information about features such as continents, countries, mountain ranges, cities, and streets. A map may also give information about specific features such as seasonal temperatures, political boundaries, aerial views, types of products raised or manufactured, and history. A map may even represent a fictional place.

> *Work individually or in groups to find examples of some or all of the types of maps below. Share what you have found with your class.*

* **a product map,** showing specific crops, animals, and /or manufactures products.

* **a seasonal temperature map,** contrasting at least two times of the year

* **a globe,** giving a round view of the world

* **a road map,** showing highways, landmarks, cities, points of interest, etc.

* **a city map,** detailing the streets and buildings in a city

* **a street map,** enlarging a specific area of a city

* **an aerial map,** depicting flight patterns for planes

* **a population map,** outlining the areas of population concentration

* **a historical map,** presenting information about a geographical area from a time in history

* **a political boundary map,** showing the borders of states, countries, or provinces

* **a weather map,** giving an idea of the rain, snow, wind, and sunshine in a specific area

* **an evaluation map,** contrasting the highs and lows of a land

* **a state, country,** or **province map,** showing the capital and major cities

* **a national park map** (or other point-of-interest map), detailing features about the point of interest

* **a fictional map,** recreating something from a fantasy world

Early Maps

Early maps were made in materials such as dirt, bark, clay, and stone. They helped people know more about where they were or wanted to be.

As time went on, mapmakers wanted to make their maps more accurate. Using the sun and stars to guide them, they started to draw places in relation to other places. For example, one town was closer to the sun at sunrise than another town was. The lake was toward the North Star. The forest was on the sunset side of the canyon. Early mapmakers began to place things according to direction.

On a separate piece of paper, make a map as the early mapmakers might have done. Map five places in your town using the position of the sun to guide you. For example, your house might be one the sunrise side of the city park. If you face the sunset while standing in your front yard, your school might be on your left side. It might help to be outside as you plan your map!

As early mapmakers understood and used direction more, maps became a more accurate picture of the world in which people lived. People began to use maps more. They needed to have maps that could be carried more easily than the maps made on clay or tree bark. Maps were made on animal skins and later on cloth. The word map comes from the Latin word mappa, which means napkin or cloth.

When paper was discovered, maps were easily made, carried, and share, making the world more known to all who could read them.

The Parts of a Map

Nearly all maps have parts that are the same. You will learn about each of these parts as you complete the map activities in this book.

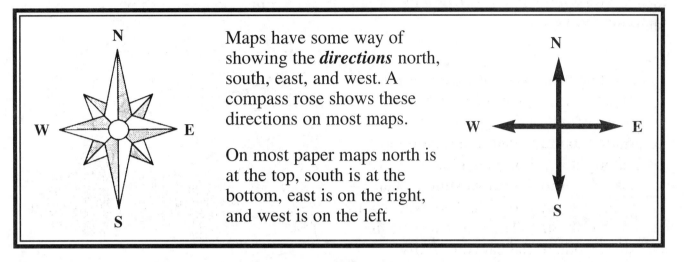

Maps have some way of showing the *directions* north, south, east, and west. A compass rose shows these directions on most maps.

On most paper maps north is at the top, south is at the bottom, east is on the right, and west is on the left.

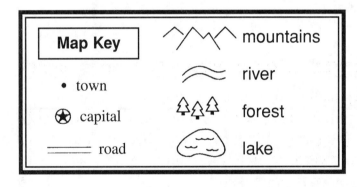

Maps use *symbols* that stand for things that are drawn on the map. These symbols are explained in a map key.

Scales are used on maps as a tool for measuring distance. Mapmakers usually draw things smaller than they really are.

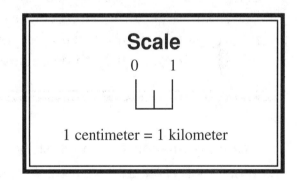

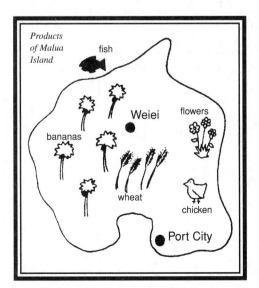

Maps have *titles* and *labels*. A *title* tells us what the map is about. *Labels* tell us what things on the map are.

Find three different maps. Identify the five parts of a map on each map you find.

Cardinal Points

There are four directions that are of prime importance when we learn our way around the world in which we live. These directions are north, south, east, and west, and they are sometimes referred to as the four cardinal points. Cardinal points are shown on maps by the use of a compass rose.

There are several ways to make a compass rose.

North and South indicators are often longer than east and west indicators.

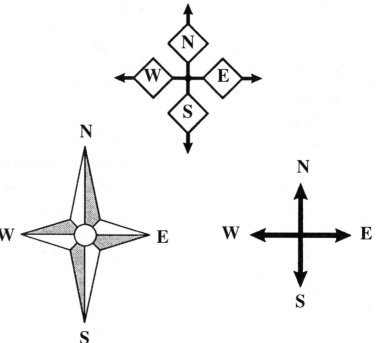

In the boxes below, draw each type of compass rose shown. Label each of the cardinal points.

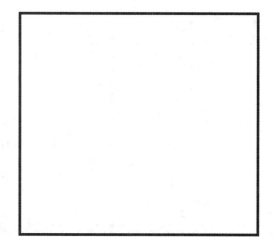

Be creative! In the box to the right, design your own compass rose. Label your cardinal points. North must be on the top.

Intermediate Points

You are familiar with the four cardinal points. But there are times when directions can not be given using simply north, south, east, or west. You need to be able to show points that come between the four primary directions. *Intermediate points* give a mapmaker just such a tool.

Study this compass rose.

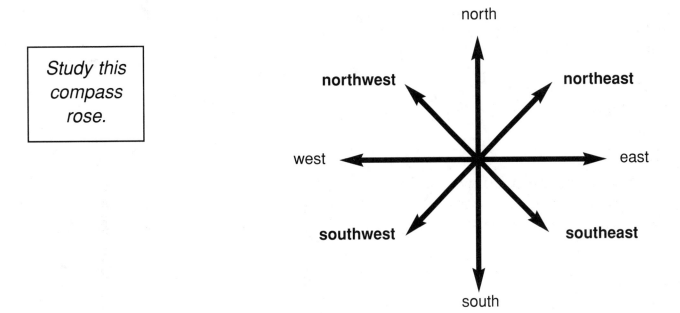

As you can see, the new direction words are made by combining the names of the cardinal points.

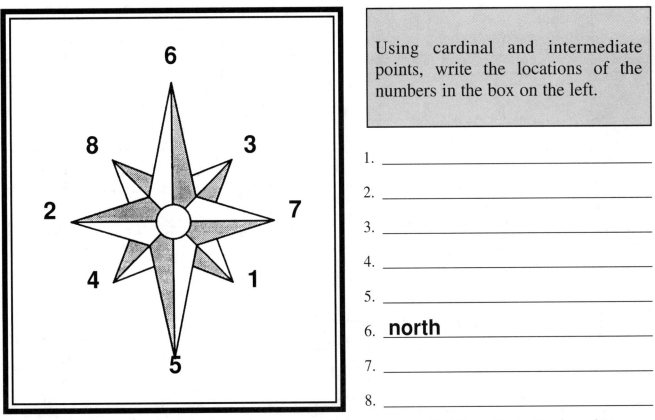

Using cardinal and intermediate points, write the locations of the numbers in the box on the left.

1. _____
2. _____
3. _____
4. _____
5. _____
6. **north** _____
7. _____
8. _____

Can You Find Home?

You are lost. Can you find your home by following the directions in the box below?

1. Begin in the most northwest home.
2. Move three houses east.
3. Move one house south.
4. Move two houses southwest.
5. Move one house west.
6. Move three houses northeast.
7. Move two houses southeast.
8. Move five houses west.
9. Move two houses north.
10. Move three houses southeast.

Follow these directions. Color each of the houses you touch red. Color your home a different color.

Label this compass rose.

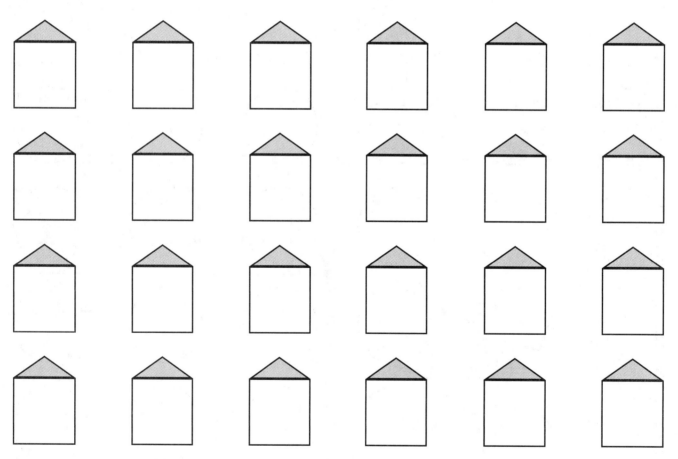

Can you rewrite the directions using fewer steps?

_____

_____

Compass Route

Use the points on a compass rose to move from the shaded circle to the striped circle. There are two rules you must follow as you write your directions.

    Rule 1: You may not move more than two circles at a time.

    Rule 2: You may not move in the same direction as you did in the previous step.

Write your directions on a separate piece of paper. Make two sets of directions.

    Set 1: Get from the shaded circle to the striped circle in as few steps possible.

    Set 2: Get from the shaded circle to the stripped circle in twelve or more steps.

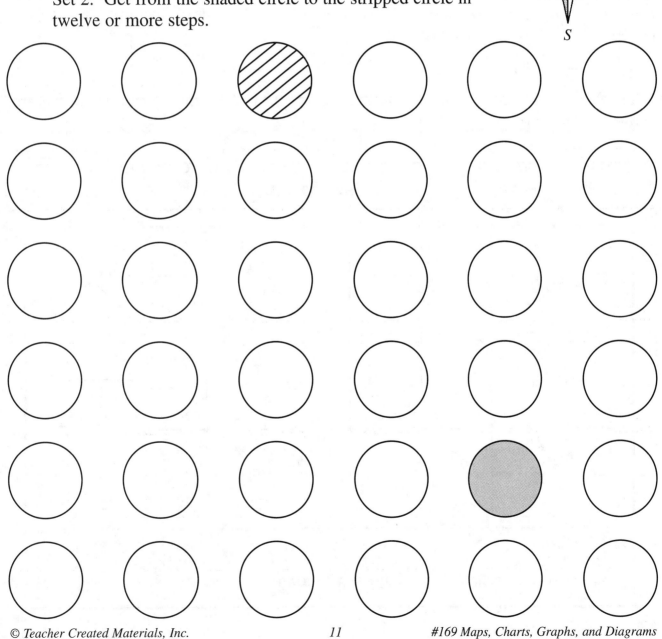

Symbols

A symbol is a mark or drawing that stands for something else.

> ### Draw symbols for these words in the boxes below them.

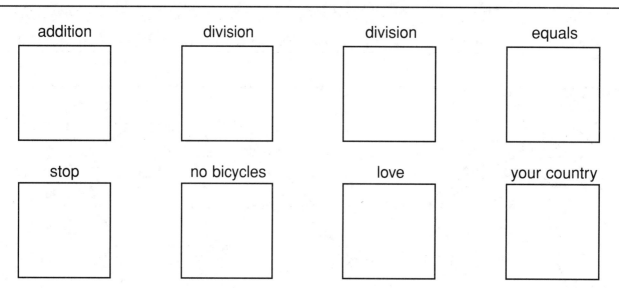

addition

division

division

equals

stop

no bicycles

love

your country

Maps also use symbols. Symbols on the map represent the things that are in the area shown by the map.

> *Here are some common map symbols. Using the words in the box at the bottom of the page, label the symbols with the words that match.*

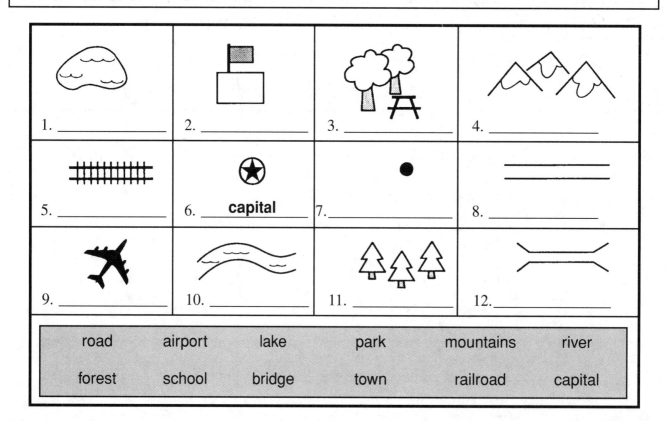

1. _____

2. _____

3. _____

4. _____

5. _____

6. **capital** _____

7. _____

8. _____

9. _____

10. _____

11. _____

12. _____

| road | airport | lake | park | mountains | river |
| forest | school | bridge | town | railroad | capital |

I've Got the Key!

Mapmakers draw the symbols they use in a *map key*. The map key explains what each symbol represents.

> *Look at this map and the map key. Use it to answer the questions below.*

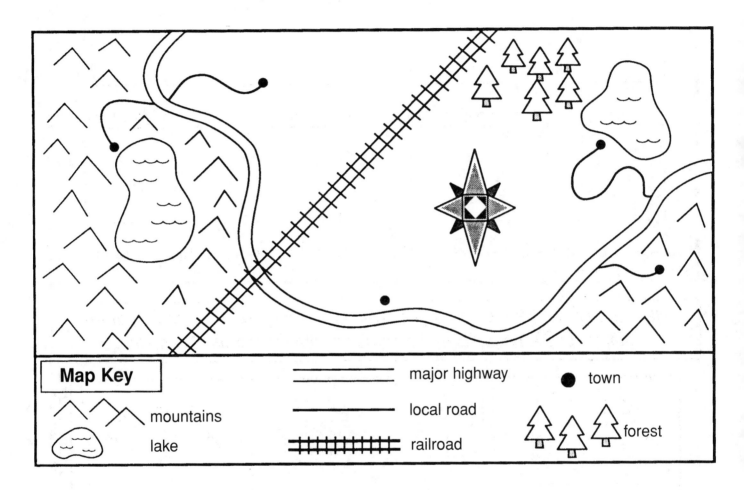

Answer true or false. If it is false, write the correct answer on the back of this paper.

1. _____ A railroad track runs southwest to northeast.

2. _____ Mountains cover the northern section of the map.

3. _____ A lake and a forest are in the southeast.

4. _____ All towns can be reached by the major highway.

5. _____ Two towns are by lakes and two towns are in the mountains.

6. _____ There are no towns along the railroad track.

7. _____ There is a large forest east of the lake and west of the railroad.

8. _____ The southernmost town is next to the major highway.

Your Map, Our Key

Using the symbols in the map key on this page, design your own map. You must use each of the symbols at least once. Draw a compass rose on your map, too.

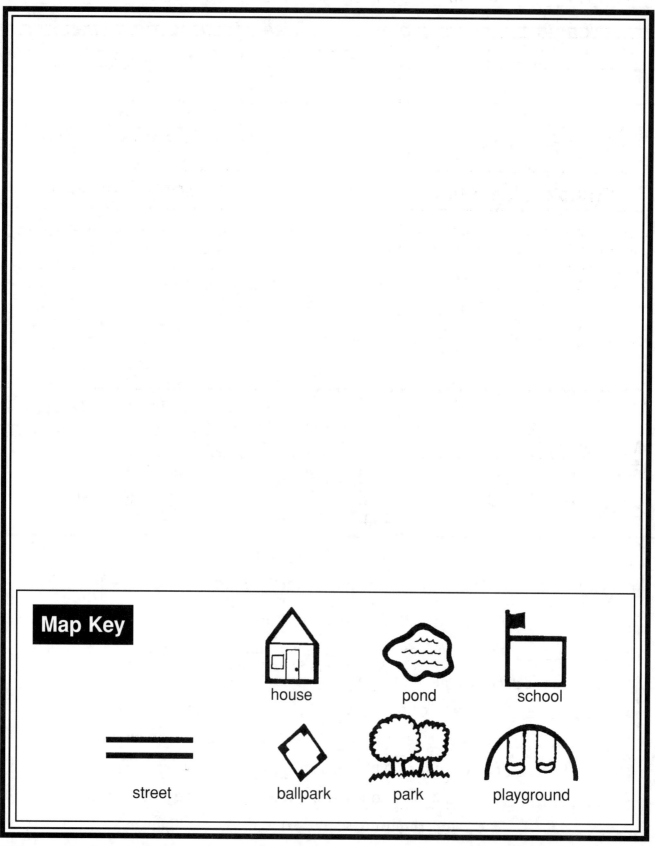

Scale

Mapmakers can make things on a map larger or smaller than they really are. They can do this by using a *map scale*. A map scale shows us a way to measure distance. We are told by the scale what kind of measurement equals what kind of distance.

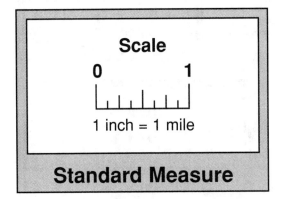

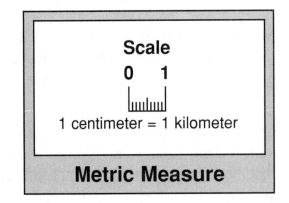

Look at this scale. One inch stands for 1 mile. If a road was 5 miles long, it would be shown on the map as 5 inches. If it was 10 miles long, it would be shown as 10 inches.

Look at this scale. One centimeter stands for 1 kilometer. If a road was 5 kilometers long, it would be shown on the map as 5 centimeters. If it was 10 kilometers long, it would be shown as 10 centimeters.

Use the scales on this page to answer these questions.

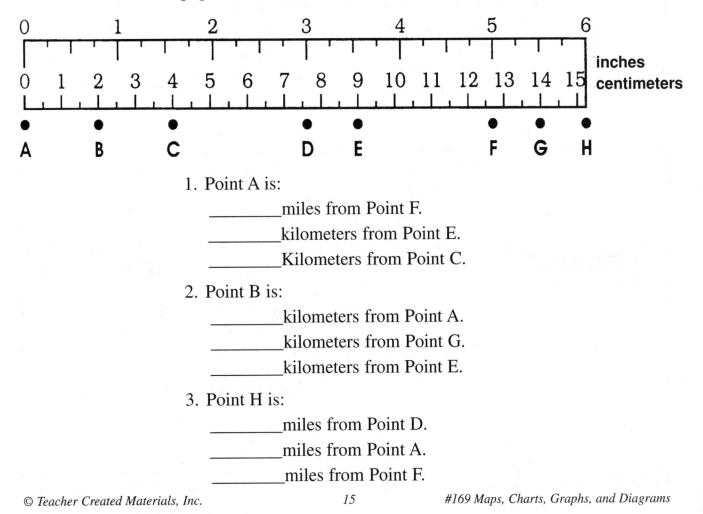

1. Point A is:

    _____miles from Point F.

    _____kilometers from Point E.

    _____Kilometers from Point C.

2. Point B is:

    _____kilometers from Point A.

    _____kilometers from Point G.

    _____kilometers from Point E.

3. Point H is:

    _____miles from Point D.

    _____miles from Point A.

    _____miles from Point F.

Measurement Choices

Measurement for a map can be given in inches, feet, and miles. This type of measurement is called *standard measure*.

Measurement for a map scale can also be given in centimeters, meters, and kilometers. This type of measurement is called *metric measure*.

On some map scales, both *standard* and *metric* measure are used. It is good to learn how to read and use both kinds of measurement systems.

When we choose a scale to use, it needs to be suited to the type of map we are making.

What do you think?

Decide on an appropriate scale to measure the size or distance of each of the following things. Use the scales in the box as you choices. Be ready to explain your choices.

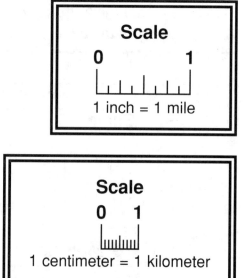

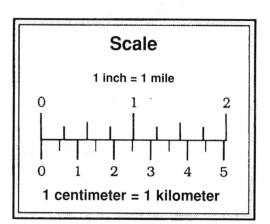

a.	1 centimeter = 1 centimeter	d.	1 inch = 1 foot
b.	1 centimeter = 1 meter	e.	1 inch = 1 mile
c.	1 centimeter = 1 kilometer	f.	1 inch = 100 miles

1. A cricket _____

2. Oregon to Texas_____

3. A bicycle race course _____

4. Your bedroom _____

5. Length of a sofa_____

6. Length of a horse's body_____

7. A swimming pool _____

8. The Mississippi River _____

9. The town park to your house _____

10. Your toes _____

How to Measure

When you measure distance using a map scale, you can measure several different ways. The easiest and most accurate way is to use a standard measure or metric measure ruler.

You can also use a piece of string, paper, the joints of your fingers, a pencil or pen, or other things that could help you mark size.

Once you have chosen your measurement instrument, place it along the imaginary or real line between the distances you want to measure.

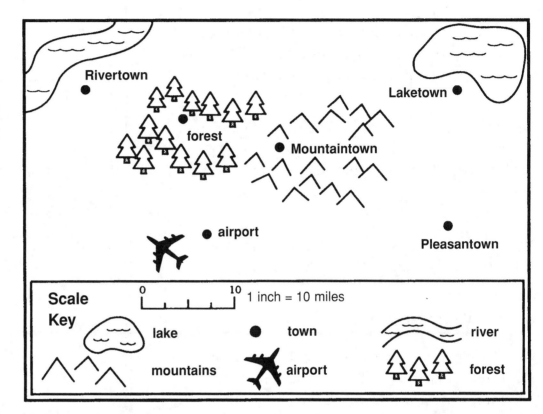

About how many miles is it between:

1. Rivertown and the airport?_____

2. Mountaintown and the forest? _____

3. Rivertown and Laketown? _____

4. Mountaintown and Pleasantown?_____

5. Laketown and Mountaintown?_____

6. Rivertown and the forest? _____

* Use your own measure to answer this question:

Is it farther from Pleasantown to Laketown or Pleasantown to Mountaintown?

_____

From Here to There

Use this map scale and a metric ruler to answer the distance questions on this page. Use the center of the dots to measure.

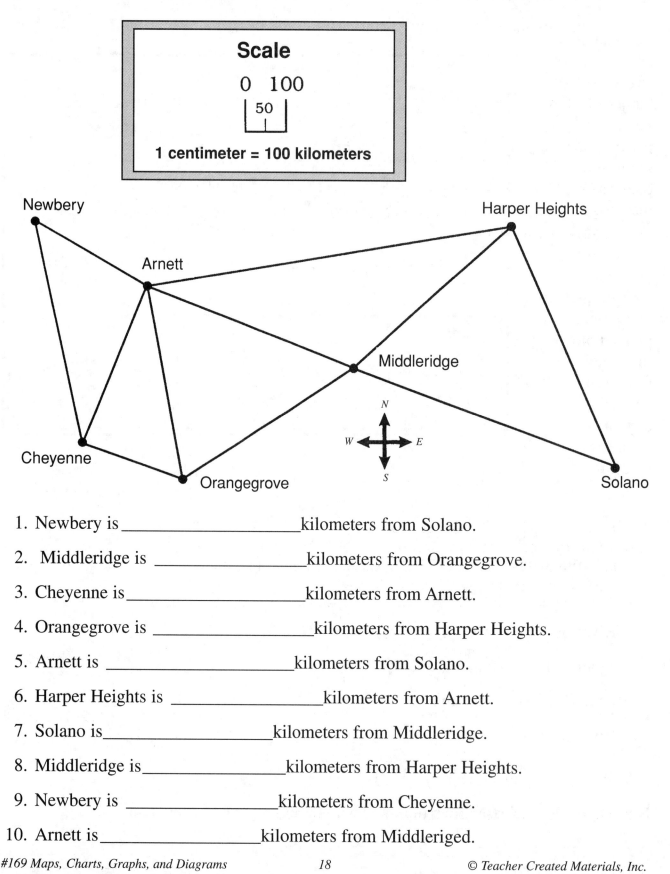

1. Newbery is _____kilometers from Solano.

2. Middleridge is _____kilometers from Orangegrove.

3. Cheyenne is_____kilometers from Arnett.

4. Orangegrove is _____kilometers from Harper Heights.

5. Arnett is _____kilometers from Solano.

6. Harper Heights is _____kilometers from Arnett.

7. Solano is_____kilometers from Middleridge.

8. Middleridge is_____kilometers from Harper Heights.

9. Newbery is _____kilometers from Cheyenne.

10. Arnett is_____kilometers from Middleriged.

In My Room

Use what you have learned about scale drawing to make a detailed map of your room. Here are some guidelines to help you in the mapmaking process.

1. Using a standard or metric measure, carefully measure the *length* and *width* of your room.

    length _____ width _____

2. Decide what a scale *inch or centimeter* will represent on your map.

    One scale _____ will equal _____

    The scaled length and width of my room is _____ by _____.

3. Draw the scaled dimensions of your room on a piece of paper.

4. Measure your closet, doors, and windows. Then, convert their measurements to scaled measurements.

	real measurement	*scaled measurement*
closet	_____	_____
doors	_____	_____
windows	_____	_____

5. Draw the closet, door, and windows on your map.

6. Measure your furniture and shelves, converting their measurements to your scale measurements. Attach a listing of your furnishings, their real measurements, and their scaled measurements to this page.

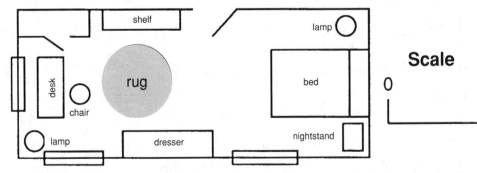

7. Add your furnishings to your map.

8. How does you map compare to the real thing?

Can I Change My Room?

You can use scale measurement to help you position things in the world around you. For example, you can use scale measurement to plan how you might want to rearrange the furnishings in your room. Here's how:

1. Draw your room according to the scale measurements you used for the "In My Room" activity. Draw only doors, closets, and windows — the things that won't change. Do not draw the furnishings.

2. Cut each furnishing to scale from colored construction paper.

3. Arrange the paper furnishings in your floor plan the way that they exist now.

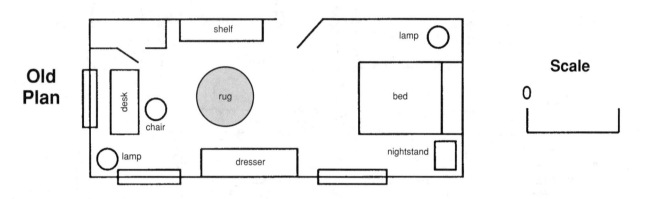

4. Rearrange the paper furnishings. What looks good? What would not work? Is the height of any of your furnishings a determining factor? (You might not want to cover up a window with shelves!)

5. Create one new arrangement of your furnishings. Attach it in place with glue or tape.

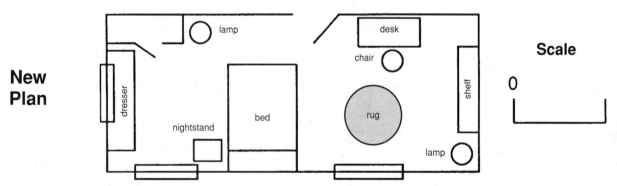

6. Compare the strengths and weaknesses of the old and new plan. Be able to explain why each floor plan "works" and/or "doesn't work."

7. Share your floor plans with your family. If you'd like to change the arrangement of your room, ask if you may.

Alberta, Canada

Alberta is one of the provinces in Canada. Can you use what you have learned about scale measurement to answer the questions about Alberta on page 22?

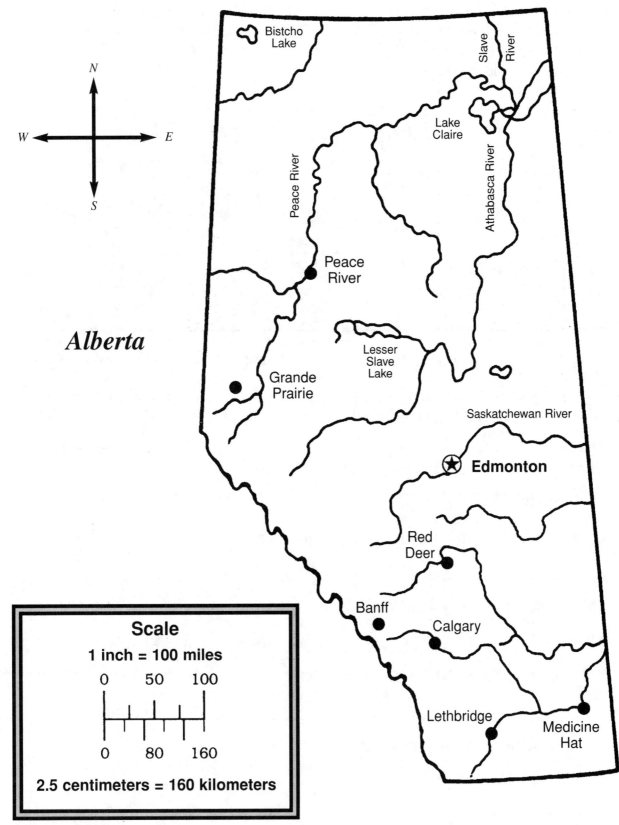

Figure It Out!

Use the map of Alberta found on page 21 and a ruler to help you answer these questions.

1. How long is the eastern edge of Alberta, measuring from north to south?

   _____ **miles**

2. What is the distance between Lake Claire and Lesser Slave Lake?

   about _____ **miles**

3. About how many kilometers is it from the town of Red Deer to the capital city of Edmonton?

   _____ **kilometers**

4. Circle the following sentences that are true about the Peace River.

   a. The Peace River flows through Alberta for at least 400 miles.

   b. The Peace River passes by the town of Peace River about 160 kilometers from Alberta's western border.

   c. The Peace River flows north for about 25 miles.

5. Fill in these blanks.

   a. Edmonton is about 250 miles from the towns of

   _____ and _____.

   b. Medicine hat is 160 kilometers from the town of_____.

   c. The _____ edge of Alberta measures about 200 miles.

   d. The distance from Calgary to the nearest border is about

   _____miles or _____kilometers.

Make up one scale question of your own!

_____

_____

Grids

A grid is an arrangement of blocks that are made by vertical and horizontal lines intersecting on a page. Numbers and letters are used on the grid to help you name the blocks.

You can find something on a grid by putting a finger of your right hand on a number and a finger on your left hand on a letter. Then, slide your fingers together until they meet. When grid points are identified, the letter is written before the number.

	1	2	3	4
A	white	yellow	orange	gold
B	pink	green	tan	red
C	blue	purple	brown	silver
D	black	ivory	gray	lavender

Try it! What color is in block C4?

_____

Use the grid to name each of the colors identified below.

A1 _____ D4 _____ B4 _____ D2 _____

C4_____ A2 _____ D1_____ C2 _____

B3_____ A4 _____ C3_____ B1 _____

D4_____ B2 _____ A3_____ C1 _____

	1	2	3
A	shaded		shaded
B		striped	shaded
C	striped	shaded	striped

Use the grid on the left to answer these questions.

Which blocks are shaded?

_____

Which blocks are striped?

_____

Which blocks are unmarked?

_____

Where in This City?

Use the grid on the city map to find the places listed at the bottom of the page. Write the letter before the number of each place you find.

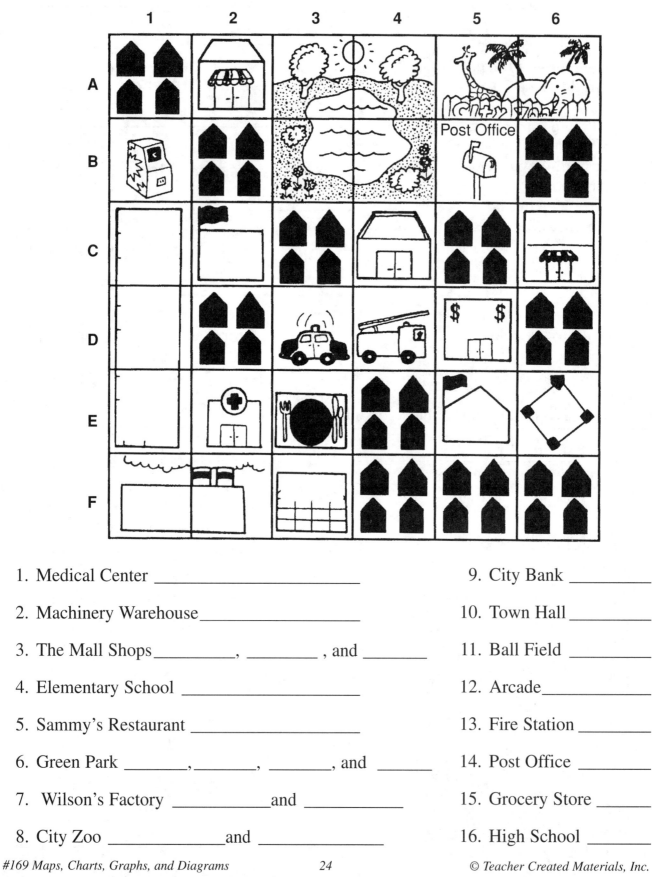

1. Medical Center _____

2. Machinery Warehouse_____

3. The Mall Shops_____, _____ , and _____

4. Elementary School _____

5. Sammy's Restaurant _____

6. Green Park _____,_____, _____, and _____

7. Wilson's Factory _____and _____

8. City Zoo _____and _____

9. City Bank _____

10. Town Hall _____

11. Ball Field _____

12. Arcade_____

13. Fire Station _____

14. Post Office _____

15. Grocery Store _____

16. High School _____

Map Titles and Labels

Maps have titles that explain what is shown on the map.

Color the title of the map we would use to discover the products grown, raised, and mined in Argentina.

Population of Argentina	**Argentina**	**Products of Argentina**	**Temperature Variations in Argentina**

Write a good title for each of these maps.

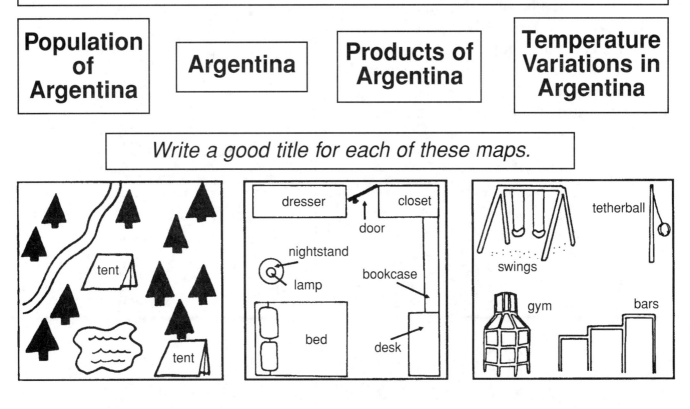

_____   _____   _____

Maps have labels that tell us names of places and things.

Use this map to answer the following questions.

1. What is the capital of Indiana? _____

2. What are three cities south of the capital?

   _____ _____ _____

3. What two cities are in the most northern part of Indiana? _____ _____

4. What city is almost in the center of Indiana?

   _____

5. What city is in the southwestern part of

   Indiana? _____

Globes

Globe

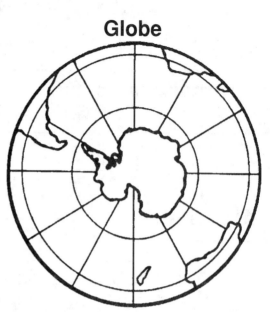

A *globe* is a model of the Earth that is round like a ball. Because the Earth is round instead of flat, a globe gives us a truer picture of what the Earth is really like. The distances and directions on a flat map are distorted because the lands near the North and South Poles are stretched out of shape. For example, compare Antarctica on the South Pole globe view to the right with Antarctica on the flat world map below. A globe represents all parts of the Earth's surface in a way that is true to scale.

Flat Map

If a globe is mounted on a center axis, it can show how the Earth rotates.

What is one continent you can see all of on the globe to the right?

_____

What continent could you see all of next if you rotated this globe to the left?

_____

Globe On Axis

Oceans and Continents

The largest areas of land in the world are called continents. There are seven continents, and their combined area covers about 30% of the world's surface.

The largest areas of water in the world are called oceans. There are four main oceans. These oceans, along with the other bodies of water in the world, cover about 70% of its surface.

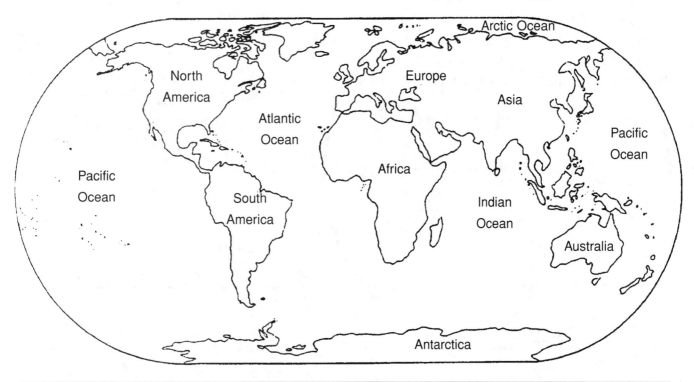

Use an almanac or other reference source to complete these questions.

1. What is the area of each continent?

   Africa _____   Antarctica _____

   Asia_____   Australia _____

   Europe_____   North America _____

   South America _____

2. What is the area of each ocean?

   Pacific Ocean _____   Atlantic Ocean _____

   Indian Ocean_____   Arctic Ocean_____

On the back of this paper, order the continents and oceans from largest to smallest.

The Equator and Hemispheres

The Earth is divided into two parts by an imaginary line called the *equator*. The part of the Earth that is north of the equator is called the *Northern Hemisphere*. The part of the Earth that is south of the equator is called the *Southern Hemisphere*.

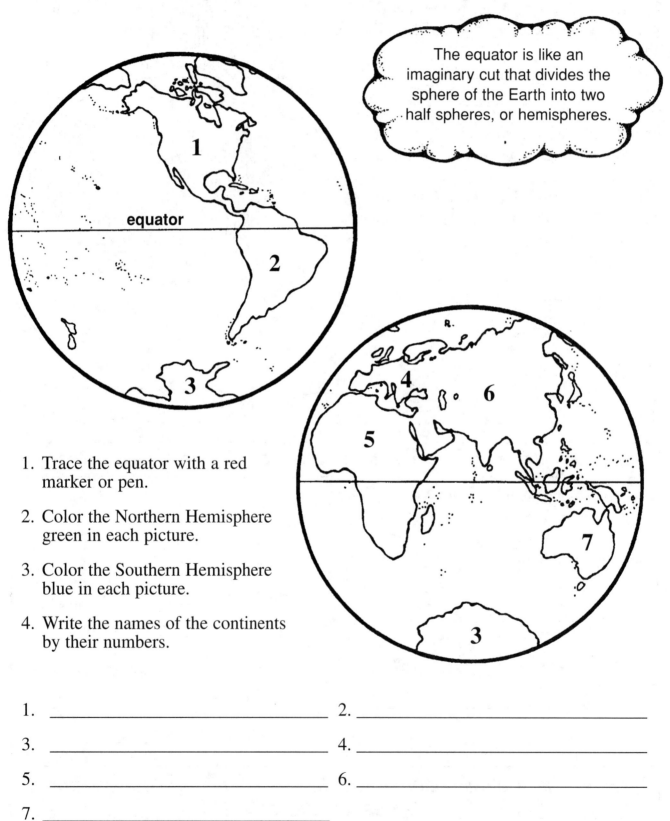

The equator is like an imaginary cut that divides the sphere of the Earth into two half spheres, or hemispheres.

1. Trace the equator with a red marker or pen.

2. Color the Northern Hemisphere green in each picture.

3. Color the Southern Hemisphere blue in each picture.

4. Write the names of the continents by their numbers.

1. _____   2. _____

3. _____   4. _____

5. _____   6. _____

7. _____

The Poles and Hemispheres

Just as the Earth is divided into a northern half and a southern half by an imaginary line called the equator, it is also divided into a western half and an eastern half by two imaginary lines that run from the *North Pole* to the *South Pole*.

The line that connects the North Pole and the South Pole on one side of the Earth is called the *prime meridian*. It runs through a place called Greenwich (pronounced Gren'ich), which is in England. The line that connects the North Pole and South Pole on the opposite side of the Earth is called the *International Date Line*. Both lines are part of the same circle that goes around the Earth.

North Pole

Eastern Hemisphere

Western Hemisphere

South Pole

Western Hemisphere

Eastern Hemisphere

The half of the Earth that is west of the prime meridian is called the *Western Hemisphere*. The half of the Earth that is east of the prime meridian is called the *Eastern Hemisphere*.

Name the continents that are in the Western Hemisphere.

1. _____   2. _____

3. _____

Name the continents that are mostly in the Eastern Hemisphere.

4. _____   5. _____

6. _____   7. _____

8. _____

On the back of this paper, write the names of five *countries* in the Western Hemisphere and five *countries* in the Eastern Hemisphere. Use a world map to help you.

Where Is It?

Use the hemisphere maps on this page to help you locate the correct hemispheres for the places listed below.

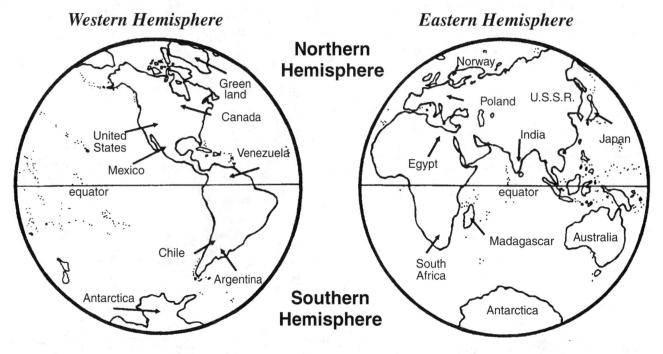

Hemisphere Location Chart

Place	Hemisphere(Northern or Southern)	Hemisphere(Eastern or Western)
1. South Africa		
2. Norway		
3. Venezuela		
4. Canada		
5. Japan		
6. Mexico		
7. U.S.S.R.		
8. Egypt		
9. United States		
10. Argentina		
11. Poland		
12. Greenland		
13. India		
14. Chile		
15. Madagascar		
16. Australia		

Latitude and Longitude

You can find places in the world by knowing how to read *latitude* and *longitude* lines. Latitude and longitude lines (also called *meridian* lines) are imaginary lines that divide the Earth. You have already learned two of these lines — the equator and the prime meridian. The equator is the main line of latitude. The prime meridian is the main line of longitude.

Latitude lines run from west to east. They measure distances north and south of the equator.

The equator cuts the world into north and south latitude. The equator is marked 0 degrees. The latitude lines north of the equator are marked N (degrees north) and the latitude lines south of the equator are marked S (degrees south).

Longitude lines run from north to south, pole to pole. They measure distances west and east of the prime meridian.

The prime meridian cuts the world into west and east longitudes. The longitude lines west of the prime meridian are marked W (degrees west) and the longitude lines east of the prime meridian are marked E (degrees east).

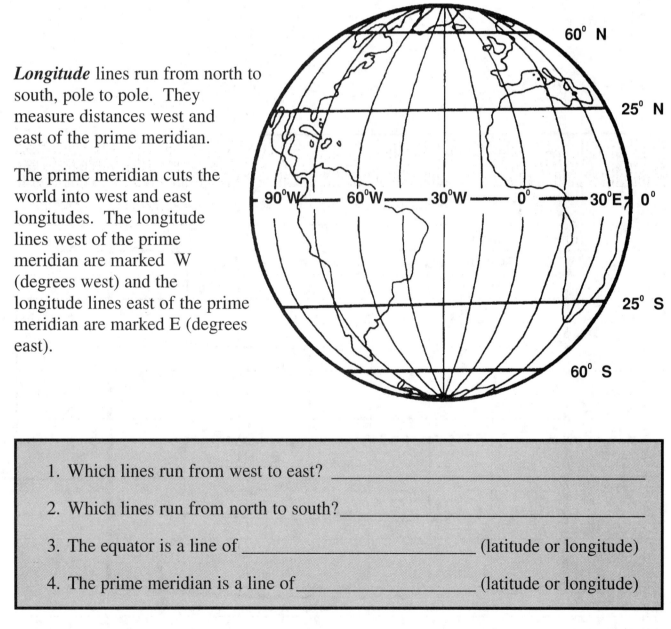

1. Which lines run from west to east? _____

2. Which lines run from north to south?_____

3. The equator is a line of _____ (latitude or longitude)

4. The prime meridian is a line of_____ (latitude or longitude)

How Many Degrees?

The intersection of the Earth's latitude and longitude lines form a grid. All of these lines have degree markings. If you know the degrees of latitude and longitude of a certain place, you can easily find it on a map.

The map of Colorado below shows the latitude and longitude lines that divide the state. Use the map to answer these questions.

Which city is near:

1. 39° N, 109° W?_____

2. 41° N, 103° W?_____

3. 40° N, 105° W?_____

4. 38° N, 102° W?_____

5. 37° N, 108° W?_____

6. 39° N, 105° W?_____

7. 39° N, 107° W?_____

8. 37° N, 103° W?_____

9. 41° N, 108° W?_____

10. 39° N, 102° W?_____

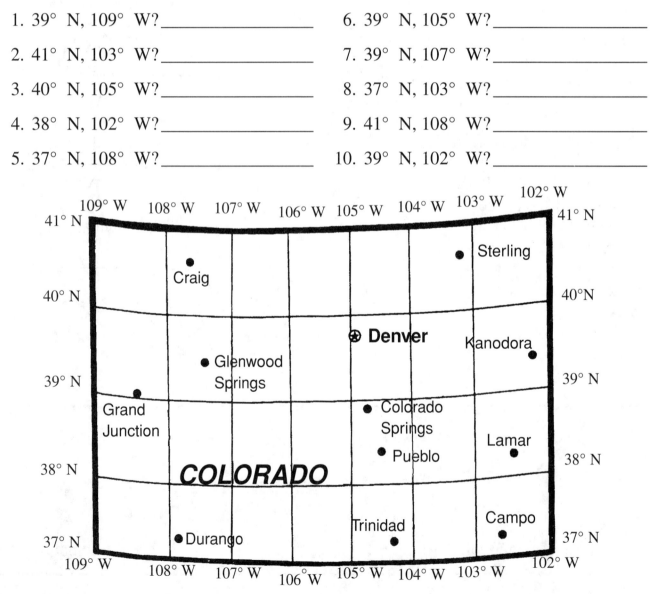

Physical Maps

A *physical map* shows the elevation, vegetation, or some other physical feature of the land.

Sometimes the physical features of the land are shown by colors and sometimes they are shown by shading.

Look at this map of Maine

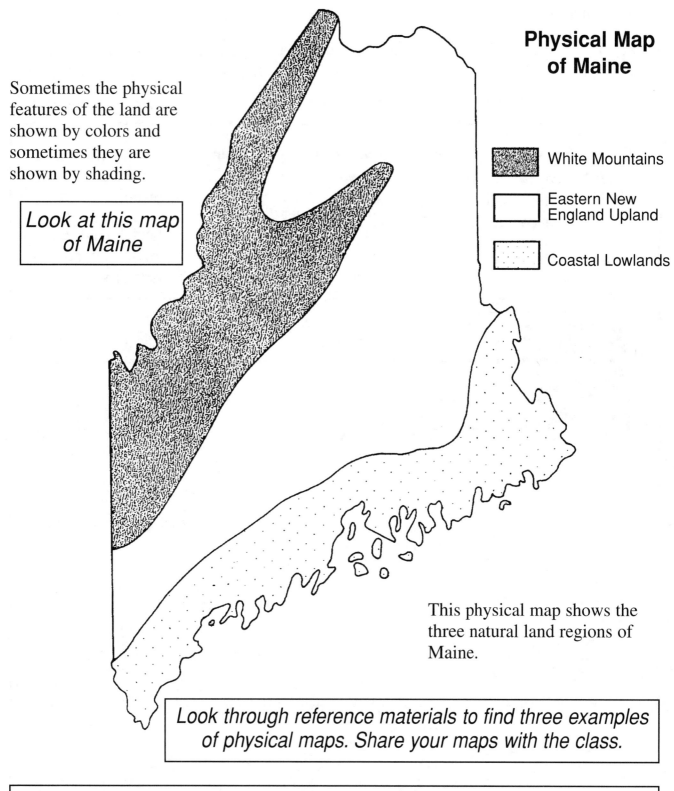

Physical Map of Maine

White Mountains

Eastern New England Upland

Coastal Lowlands

This physical map shows the three natural land regions of Maine.

Look through reference materials to find three examples of physical maps. Share your maps with the class.

Make a physical map of the state, province, or country in which you live. Show the elevation of the land. Don't forget a key.

Landforms

Physical maps can show us the *form* of the land. We can learn the location of mountains, rivers, lakes, plateaus, valleys, and other features of the land by studying a physical map of landforms.

Using this key and the landform definitions found on this page, create a place that has all the landforms described below. Coordinate the colors in your key with your landforms. Don't forget to name you place!

Definitions			
	lake: enclosed body of water	**plain:**	open, flat land, lower than a plateau
mountain: high, steep-sided land	**river:** running water in a path that has cut the land	**valley:**	land that is much lower than the land around it
plateau: high, flat land			

Landform Key

	mountain		river
	plateau		plain
	lake		valley

Boundary Search

The lines that show where countries, provinces, states, and territories are divided are called *boundary lines.*

On this map of Central America, find the boundary lines for each country. Use reference material to help you name the countries. Then color each country according to the color specified in the chart below.

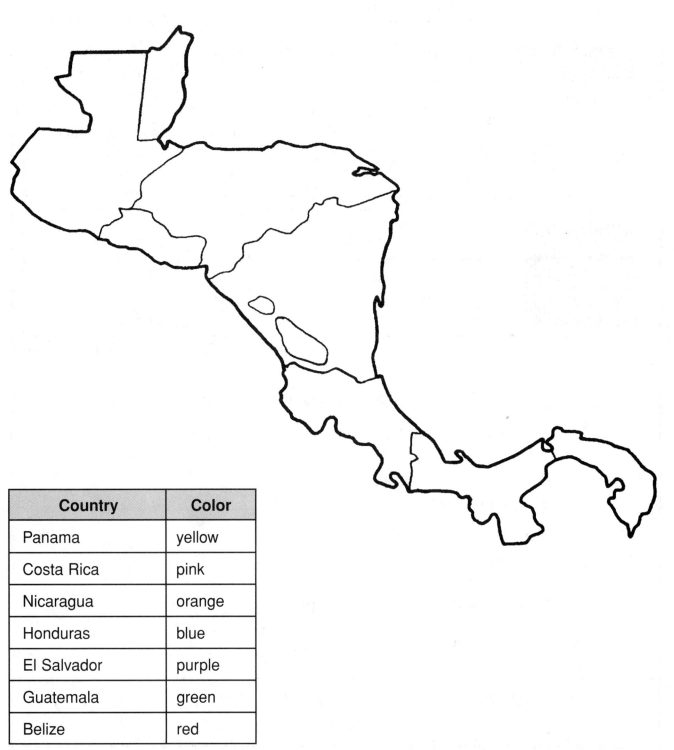

Country	Color
Panama	yellow
Costa Rica	pink
Nicaragua	orange
Honduras	blue
El Salvador	purple
Guatemala	green
Belize	red

Political Maps

One type of map that uses boundary lines is called a ***political map***. A political map gives us information about country, province, state, and county boundaries as well as information about cities, towns, highways, roads, forest areas, and points of interest. Political maps also show oceans, rivers, and lakes, but they do not show the elevations of the land area as physical maps do.

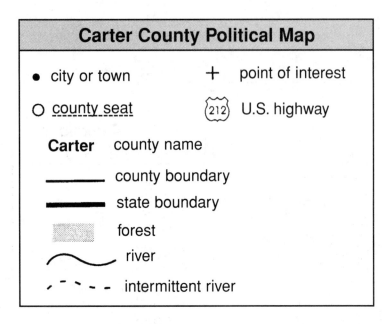

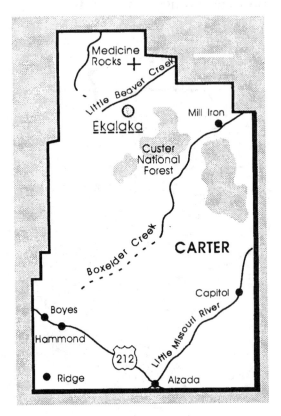

Use this political map of Carter County, Montana, to answer the questions below.

1. Which sides of Montana's border does Carter County help form? _____

   _____

2. What is the name of the county seat? _____

3. Through what three cities does the U.S. highway pass? _____

   _____

4. Name the intermittent river in Carter County. _____

5. What is the point of interest in this county? _____

On a separate piece of paper, make a political map of the county in which you live.

Historical Maps

There is another type of map that makes sue of boundary lines. These maps are called *historical maps* and show something about the history of an area.

At the time of Columbus, there were about 300 Native American tribes in North America. These tribes are often divided into seven groups: Woodland, Plains, Southwestern, California-Intermountain, Pacific Coast, Far North, and Middle American.

Use this historical map to answer questions about the Native Americans of early North America.

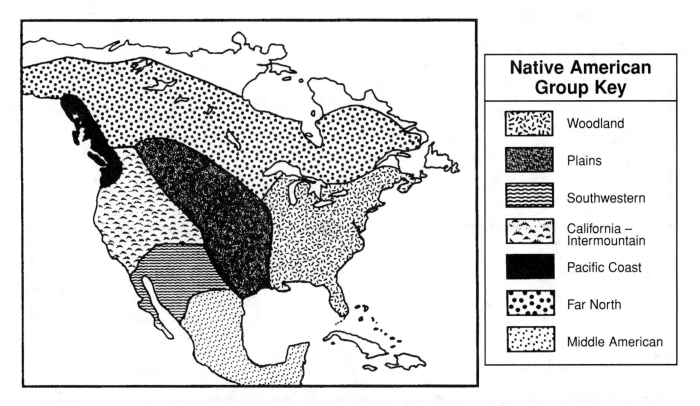

1. What group of Native Americans covered the largest North American area?

_____

2. What group of Native Americans were both in Mexico and the United States?

_____

3. What group of Native American covered the smallest North American area?

_____

4. What Native Americans were the early inhabitants of North Dakota, South Dakota, Nebraska, and Kansas?

_____

Road Maps

Road maps show the types of roads that are in a specific area. They also tell use other things we may need to know as we plan for travel, such as the distances from town to town, the location of rest areas, and the availability of scenic routes.

> *After you read this map, answer the questions at the bottom of the page.*

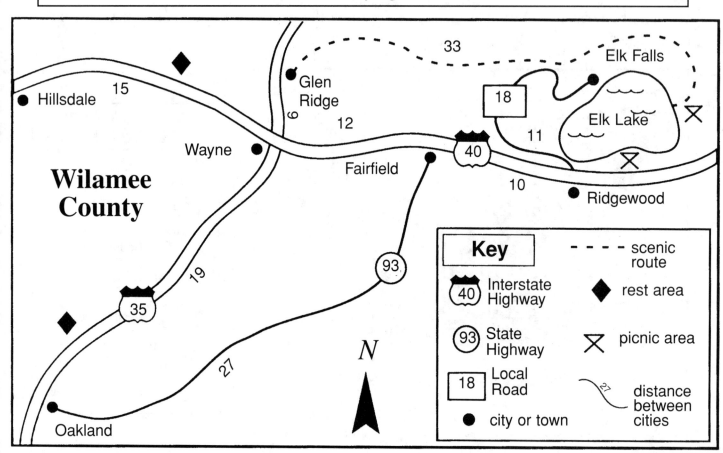

1. Near what highways are the rest areas? _____

2. If you travel on State Highway 93, what is the distance from Oakland to Fairfield?

   _____

3. Interstate Highways 35 and 40 intersect at what city? _____

4. There is a scenic route that ends at the East side of Elk Lake. Where does it begin?_____ How long is it? _____

5. What is the distance from Hillsdale to:

   a. Wayne? _____   b. Ridgewood? _____

   c. Fairfield? _____   c. Elk Falls? _____

How Many Miles to Go?

Use the map on this page to answer the questions.

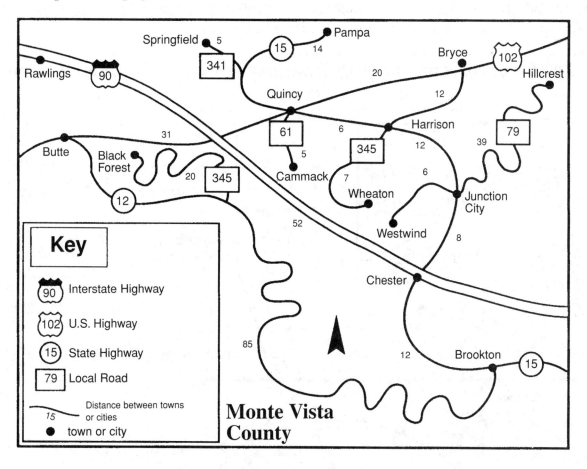

1. You are in Butte. How far do you have to travel to:

    a. Quincy _____   b. Pampa?_____   c. Harrison?_____

    d. Hillcrest? _____   e. Bryce? _____   f. Brookton? _____

2. You are in Westwind. How far do you have to travel to:

    a. Junction City? _____   b. Chester? _____   c. Bryce?_____

    d. Hillcrest? _____   e. Rawlings? _____   f. Cammack?_____

3. You are in Hillcrest. How far do you have to travel to:

    a. Rawlings? _____   b. Bryce? _____   c. Wheaton? _____

    d. Brookton? _____   e. Westwind? _____   f. Pampa? _____

Challenge: Describe the route that would be fastest from Butte to Brookton.

_____

Why?_____

Population Maps

A *population map* shows the areas in which people live. This map shows the average number of people who live in certain areas of California. It is called a *population density* map.

Use the map to answer these questions. Write your answers on another piece of paper.

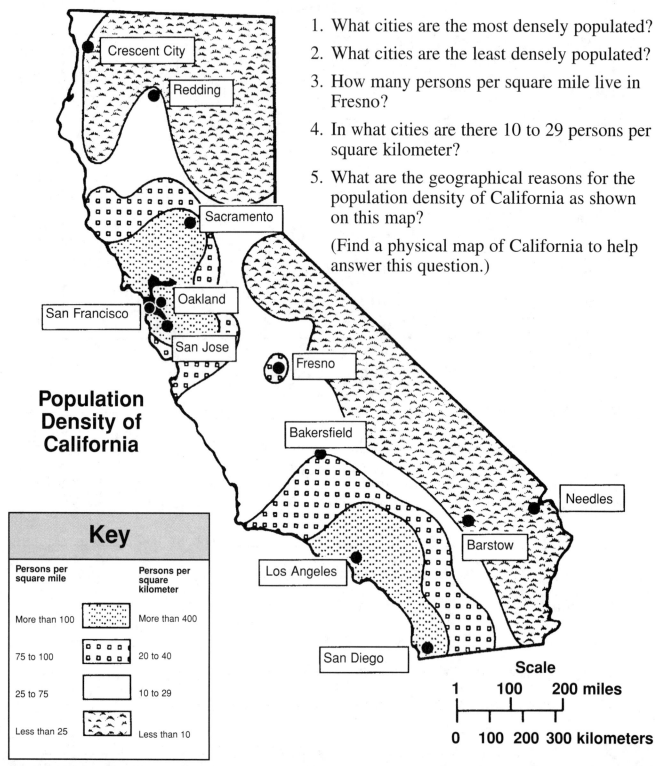

1. What cities are the most densely populated?
2. What cities are the least densely populated?
3. How many persons per square mile live in Fresno?
4. In what cities are there 10 to 29 persons per square kilometer?
5. What are the geographical reasons for the population density of California as shown on this map?

   (Find a physical map of California to help answer this question.)

Population Density of California

Key

Persons per square mile		Persons per square kilometer
More than 100		More than 400
75 to 100		20 to 40
25 to 75		10 to 29
Less than 25		Less than 10

Crescent City
Redding
Sacramento
Oakland
San Francisco
San Jose
Fresno
Bakersfield
Needles
Barstow
Los Angeles
San Diego

Scale

1   100   200 miles

0   100 200 300 kilometers

Product Maps

Sometimes maps can show us the types of things that are grown, raised, or mined in a certain place. These maps are called *product maps.*

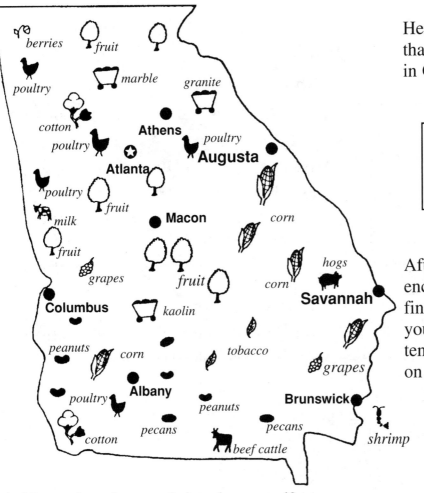

Here are some of the products that are grown, raised, or mined in Georgia.

Use the information on the map to answer the questions below.

After you have finished, use an encyclopedia or other source to find a product map of the place you live. Redraw it, selecting ten to twenty products to draw on your map.

1. Near what city are shrimp harvested?_____

2. What product is produced in great quantity near Macon? _____

3. What products are grown more in the southern part of Georgia than in the northern part? Name three.

   1. _____ 2. _____ 3. _____

4. What product is produced in the northwest corner of Georgia that is not produced in any great quantity in other locations in Georgia?

   _____

5. What food is grown between Augusta and Savannah?_____

6. What types of products are mined in the northern part of the state?

   _____

Weather Maps

Weather maps show what the weather of a specific area has been or could be. Weather patterns are shown on maps by using symbols or shading.

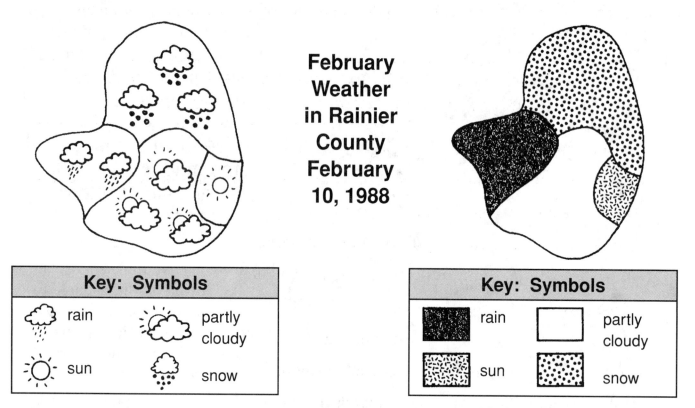

Weather maps can also show average temperatures in a specific area. Here is a map of the average January temperatures in Massachusetts.

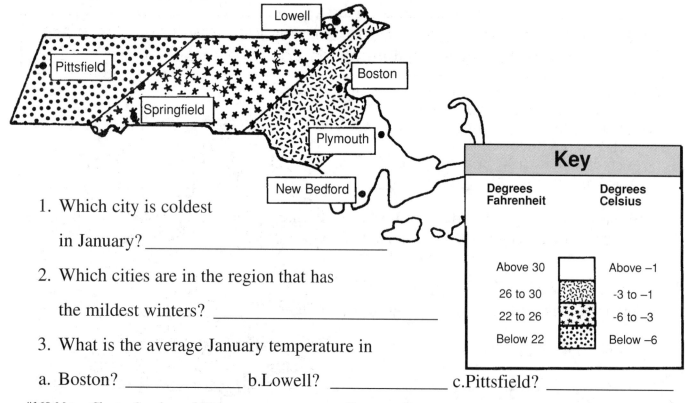

1. Which city is coldest in January? _____

2. Which cities are in the region that has the mildest winters? _____

3. What is the average January temperature in

a. Boston? _____ b.Lowell? _____ c.Pittsfield? _____

It's Your World

Maps can be made of fantasy places as well as real places. Many fiction writers make maps of the worlds they create to help a reader better understand the story. J.R.R. Tolkien's map of Wilderland in *The Hobbit* is just one of many examples of fantasy world maps.

Create a map to a fantasy world on a separate sheet of paper. Here are some suggestions to help you get started.

- Make a map of the places in a book you have read.

- Make a map that follows the path a character has followed in a book you have read.

- Design a map of the perfect place for you.

- Create a map of a frightening world, full of dangers.

- Design a map of a world from the past or in the future.

- Make a map to a fairy-tale world.

- Design the ideal room for a person your age.

- Map out the attractions at a perfect amusement park.

- Make a map of a backyard you would like to have.

- Create a map of places you would like to write a story about.

Remember, it's you world, so make it any way you want. Here are some things to remember as you make your map.

- Include a compass rose on your map.

- Remember to draw your map to scale and include a guide for your scale.

- Include a key for any symbols you use.

- Print or write neatly as you label specific areas.

It All Adds Up!

The map skills you have learned in this book all add up! Can you read this map?

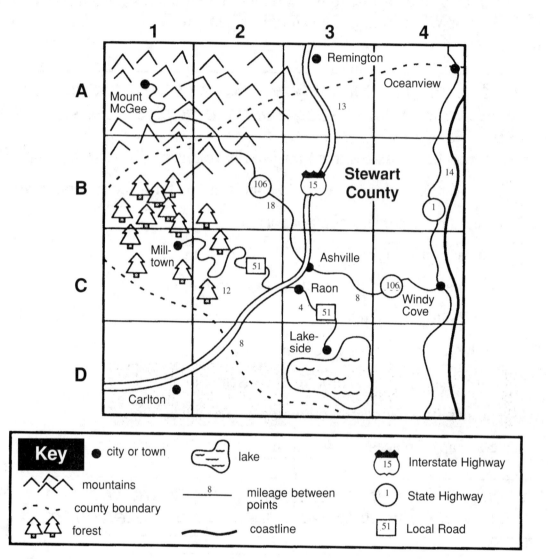

1. At what gridpoints are the following places?

a. Lakeside _____ b.Mount McGee _____ c.Ashville_____

2. What gridpoints are completely out of Stewart County? _____

3. What type of road leads from Windy Cover to Mount McGee? _____

4. Lumber products might be milled in what grid points? _____

5. What cities are not in Stewart County? _____

6. How many miles is it from:

    a. Lakeside to Milltown?_____   b. Oceanview to Ashville? _____

7. State Highway 1 parallels what kind of land? _____

What Is a Chart?

A *chart* is a visual tool that gives us an easy way to see information. Sometimes it is easier to read a chart than it is to read a paragraph. Here is an example.

Paragraph Form

Mrs. Regent asked her class of twenty-nine fourth graders to find out on which day of the week they were born. She found out that seven students were born on Sunday and four on Monday. Three students were born on Tuesday, two on Wednesday, and six on Thursday. One student was born on Friday and five on Saturday. One student was unable to find out the information.

Chart Form

| Days of the Week on Which the Students in Mrs. Regent's Class Were Born ||
Day of the Week	Number of Students
Sunday	7
Monday	4
Tuesday	3
Wednesday	2
Thursday	6
Friday	1
Saturday	5
Unable to find out information	1

Is it easier to find out this information in paragraph or chart form?_____

Why? _____

_____

How Far to New York?

Distance charts show you the distance between two places if you travel by road.

This distance chart shows the road distance between ten North American cities. Look at the chart carefully. Read it by making two finger come together to find the distance between cities. Practice. When you are comfortable using the chart, answer the questions below.

Ten City Distance Chart	Albuquerque	Boston	Chicago	Denver	Indianapolis	Los Angeles	Miami	Montreal	New York City
Boston	2172		963	1949	906	2779	1504	318	206
Chicago	1281	963		996	181	2054	1329	828	802
Denver	417	1949	996		1058	1059	2037	1815	1771
Indianapolis	1266	906	181	1058		2073	1148	840	713
Los Angeles	807	2779	2054	1059	2073		2687	2873	2786
Miami	1938	1504	1329	2037	1148	2687		1654	1308
Montreal	2087	318	8287	1815	840	2873	1654		378
New York City	1979	206	802	1771	713	2786	1308	378	
Seattle	1440	2976	2013	1307	2194	1131	3273	2685	2815

Find the distance between these cities:

1. Los Angeles and New York: _____

2. Seattle and Albuquerque: _____

3. Boston and New York City: _____

4. Denver and Miami; _____

5. New York City and Chicago: _____

6. Montreal and Indianapolis: _____

7. Chicago and Miami: _____

8. Indianapolis and Denver: _____

9. Montreal and Los Angeles: _____

10. Seattle and Boston: _____

11. Chicago and Boston: _____

12. Denver and Albuquerque: _____

Use a distance chart to find the distance you live from yeach of these cities.

Calendars

A calendar is a type of chart. It is an easy way to measure and record the passage of time.

Listed below are special events John has planned for this year. Read the calendar and then answer the questions at the bottom of the page.

January	February	March
	Trip to Canada 2/6 – 2/20	See Dr. Johnson for yearly check-up 3/15 at 11:15 a.m.
April	**May**	**June**
Tony's Birthday 4/4 Marissa's Birthday 4/4/	Nick's Birthday 5/15	Trip to the East Coast 6/18 – 6/30
July	**August**	**September**
Baseball Games 7/3 7/10 7/17 7/24	Patty's Birthday 8/18	My Birthday 9/16
October	**November**	**December**
Trip to Grand Canyon 10/21 – 10/24		Holiday Party 12/17 4:00 p.m.

1. In what months are there birthdays that John wants to remember?

_____

2. In what months does he have special trips planned? _____

_____

3. In what month is his yearly check-up? _____

4. In what month does he have baseball games? _____

5. When does he have a holiday party planned? _____

*Make a calendar of your own special times to remember!

Week at a Glance

Brenda has collected a stack of tiny notes of things she has to do next week. She knows she needs to organize them in a way that will be easy to read and understand. She decides to make a calendar.

Use Brenda's notes to make her weekly calendar.

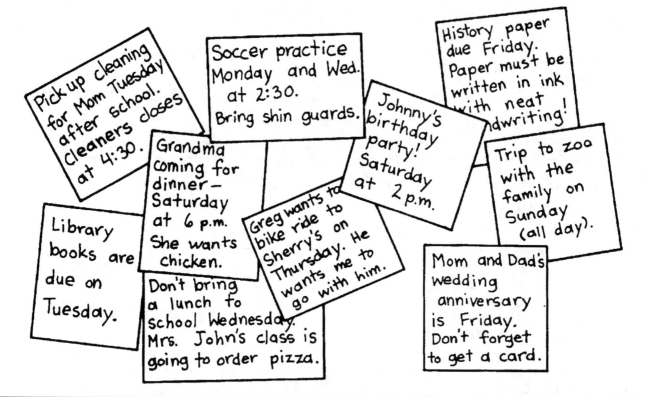

My Week October 17 – October 23	Sunday	Monday	Tuesday

Wednesday	Thursday	Friday	Saturday

Make a calendar for the thing you have to do for a week or a month. Calendars are great visual tools to use in our daily lives!

Tables

A table is a type of chart that is organized in such a way as to make information very easy to find.

Read this table about the three major classifications of rocks. Use the information in the table to answer the questions at the bottom of this page.

🪣🪣🪣🪣 Three Major Classifications of Rocks 🪣🪣🪣🪣			
Classification	rock	color	structure
Igneous Rock (forms from hardened magma)	granite	white to gray, pink to red	closely arranged medium-to-coarse crystals
	obsidian	black, sometimes with brown streaks	glassy, no crystals
	pumice	grayish-white	light, fine pores, floats on water
Sedimentary Rock (formed by hardening of plant, animal, and mineral materials)	coal	shiny to dull black	brittle, in seams or layers
	limestone	white, gray, and buff to black and red	dense, forms cliffs and may contain fossils
	shale	yellow, red, gray, green, black	dense, find particles, soft, smells like clay
Metamorphic Rock (formed by existing rock changing because of heat or pressure)	marble	many colors, often mixed	medium to coarse crystals
	quartzite	white, gray, pink, and buff	big, hard and often glassy
	schist	white, gray, red, green, black	flaky, banded, sparkles with mica

1. What is the name of the igneous rock that is black and has a glassy appearance?

_____

2. What classification of rock is most likely to contain fossils?

_____

3. To which classification do schist and marble belong?

_____

*Find other examples of tables and share them with your class.

Weights All Over

This table shows the weight of three earth people in pounds and kilograms. The weight of each person is also shown if her or she was on the Moon, Venus, Mars, or Jupiter.

Study the chart and answer the questions.

Weights on the Earth and Other Places			
	Person 1	Person 2	Person 3
Earth	200 pounds	100 pounds	50 pounds
	91 kilograms	45.5 kilograms	22.75 kilograms
The Moon	32 pounds	16 pounds	8 pounds
	15 kilograms	7.5 kilograms	3.75 kilograms
Venus	178 pounds	89 pounds	44.5 pounds
	81 kilograms	40.5 kilograms	20.25 kilograms
Mars	76 pounds	38 pounds	19 pounds
	34 kilograms	17 kilograms	8.5 kilograms
Jupiter	529 pounds	264.5 pounds	132.75 pounds
	240 kilograms	120 kilograms	60 kilograms

1. How much does a 50 pound/22.85 kilograms person weigh on:

   The Moon? _____ Mars? _____

2. How much does a 200 pound/91 kilogram person weigh on:

   Venus? _____ Jupiter? _____

3. How much does a 100 pound/45.5 kilogram person weigh on:

   The Moon? _____ Venus? _____

4. On what place do Earth people weigh most? _____

5. On what place do Earth people weigh least? _____

 • About how much would *you* weigh on each of these places? Try to figure it out!

Chart the Read-a-Thon!

Students at Hudson Elementary School have been participating in a Read-a-Thon to raise money for their school library. Each student has tallied the number of books he or she has read and is ready to collect the pledge money.

This chart represents the reading and pledging of 15 students in the Read-a-Thon. After reading the chart, answer the questions at the bottom of the page.

Hudson Elementary School Read-A-Thon: Room 3			
Student's Name	Total Books Read	Pledge per Book	Money Collected
Acevedo, Jennifer	31	10 ¢	3.10
Adams, Joseph	5	10 ¢	.50
Barton, Michael	61	5 ¢	3.05
Duran, Louis	17	15 ¢	2.55
Edwards, Marylou	47	5 ¢	2.35
Harrison, Trevor	11	25 ¢	2.75
Lee, Rebecca	40	10 ¢	4.00
Logan, Cassie	22	5 ¢	1.10
Marshall, Barbara	9	50 ¢	4.50
Peterson, David	102	5 ¢	5.10
Ross, Kathryn	58	10 ¢	5.80
Rublo, Anthony	83	5 ¢	4.15
Shea, Sharon	39	10 ¢	3.90
Tran, Alvan	14	10 ¢	1.40
Yetter, Liz	75	5 ¢	3.75
Total	614		48.00

1. Which student read the most books? _____

2. What was the highest amount of money collected by one student?_____

   Which student? _____

3. Who had the highest pledge of money per book? _____

4. Was the person who read the most books the same as the person who collected the most money? _____

5. Was the person who had the highest pledge of money per book the same as the person who collected the most money? _____

6. What was the total number of books read by these students? _____

7. How much money did these students earn for the library? _____

Would a Read-a-Thon be a good way to raise money at your school?

Flow Charts

A *flow chart* is a type of chart that shows, step-by-step, how something happens in the order it happens.

Read the flow chart showing the steps to make a pizza. Follow the arrow direction to read the chart.

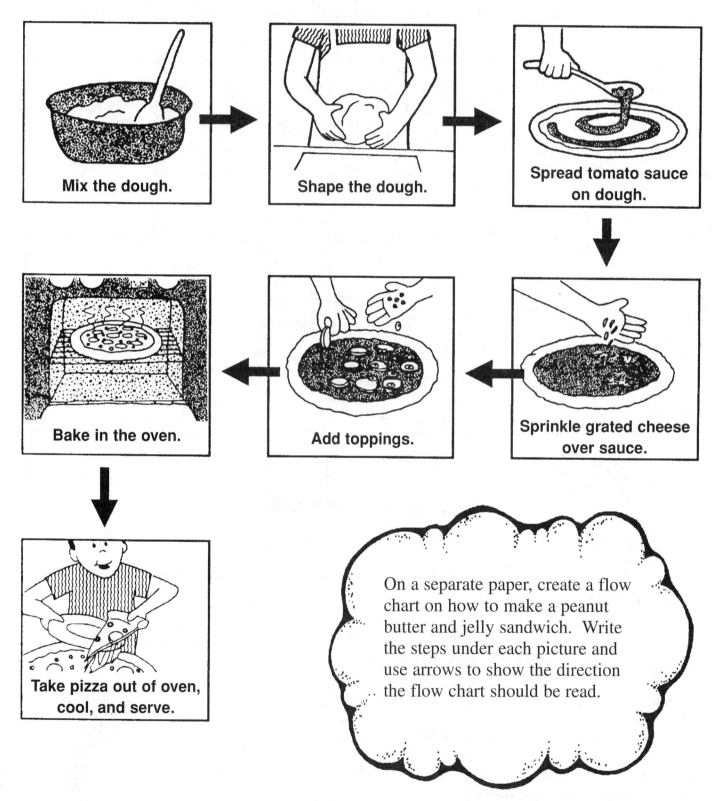

On a separate paper, create a flow chart on how to make a peanut butter and jelly sandwich. Write the steps under each picture and use arrows to show the direction the flow chart should be read.

Party Time!

Your parents planned a fantastic party for your birthday. Everyone who came to the party thought it was perfect, especially you.

What would be the perfect birthday party? Make a flow chart with written directions for at least six steps that would lead to a party's success. Use the arrows to show the order in which the steps should be taken.

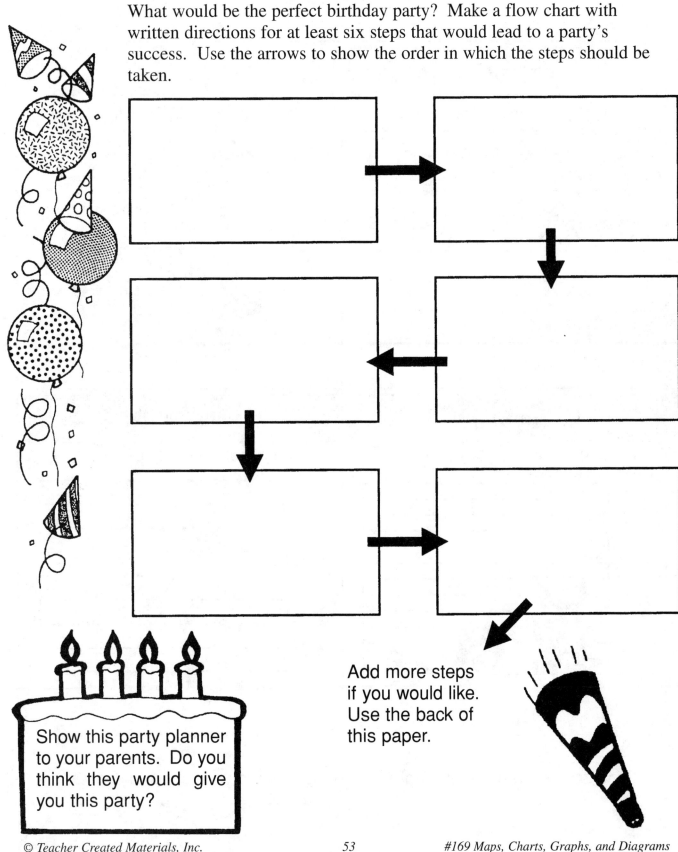

Add more steps if you would like. Use the back of this paper.

Show this party planner to your parents. Do you think they would give you this party?

What Is a Graph?

A graph is a visual tool that makes it easier for us to see information. A graph uses pictures, circles, bars, and lines to show and compare information. Shown below are the 1984 populations of three United States cities in four different types of graphs.

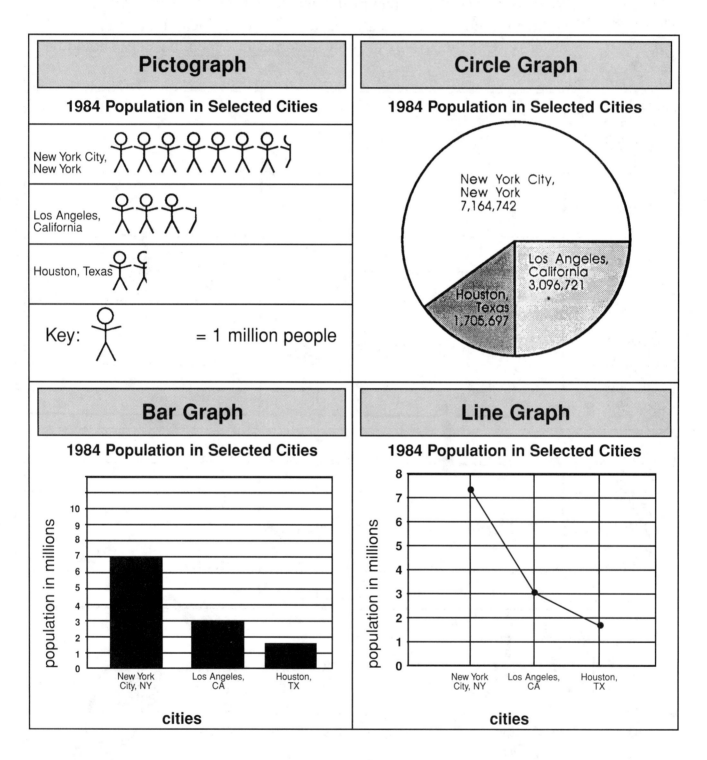

- Find some examples of graphs and bring them to your class to share.

Pictographs

One type of graph that gives us information is called a pictograph. In a pictograph, pictures are used instead of numbers.

Read this pictograph to find out the amount and types of instruments sold in April at Harmony Music Store.

April Instrument Sales at Harmony Music Store	
pianos	
flutes	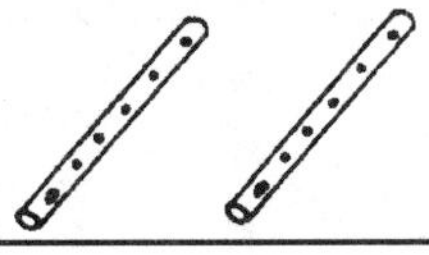
guitars	
drums	
trumpets	
Key: 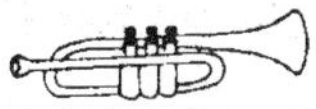 1 instrument = 5 instruments	

1. How many of each of these instruments were sold?

   pianos _____ flutes _____ guitars _____

   drums _____ trumpets _____

2. How many more guitars were sold than:

   pianos _____ flutes _____ drums _____ trumpets _____

3. Do you think the piano sales or the guitar sales brought in more money for Harmony Music Store? Explain the reason(s) for your choice.

   _____

   _____

Recycling Project

The Linsdale Elementary School Earth Kids Club worked for three months collecting recyclable products. You can see the results of their efforts in this pictograph.

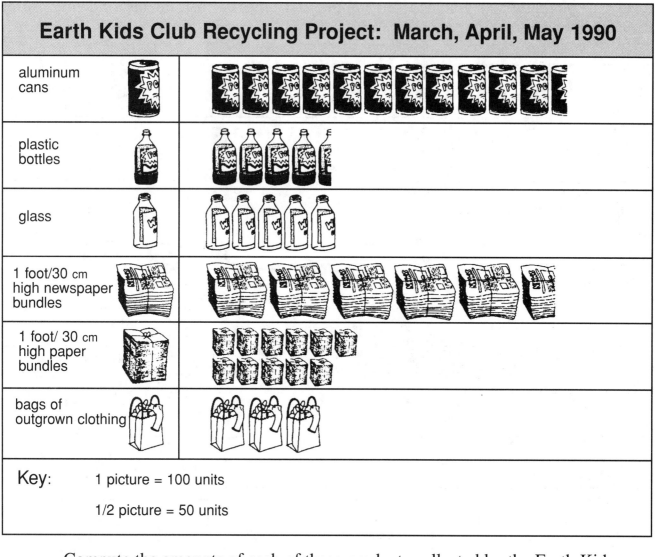

Earth Kids Club Recycling Project: March, April, May 1990

Key:
1 picture = 100 units
1/2 picture = 50 units

Compute the amounts of each of these products collected by the Earth Kids Club:

1. aluminum cans:_____   4. newspaper bundles: _____

2. plastic bottles:_____   5. paper bundles: _____

3. glass:_____   6. bags of clothing: _____

Which of these products could you and your friends help to recycle? _____

_____

_____

Responses

Your class has just been told that you will be helping the first graders at your school learn to read. Each one of you will pair up with a younger child and read with him or her once a week.

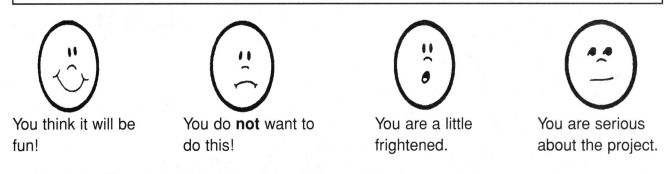

Take a class survey of the feelings the class members have about this project. Each class member must respond in one of these ways.

You think it will be fun!

You do **not** want to do this!

You are a little frightened.

You are serious about the project.

Record the class results on a pictograph, using these symbols to represent each class member's response.

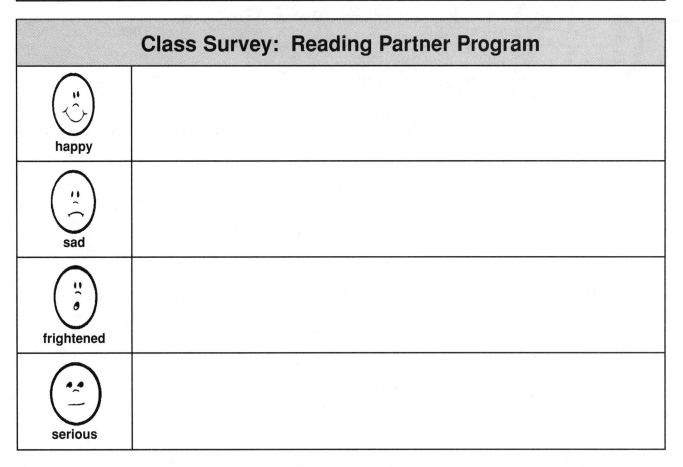

Class Survey: Reading Partner Program	
happy	
sad	
frightened	
serious	

Based on the results of this survey, would a "reading partner" program be a possibility for your class? _____ If you can, do it!

Circle Graphs

One type of graph that gives us information is called a circle graph. In a circle graph, you can show how things are divided into the parts of a whole.

Shown in this circle graph are the types and amounts of fruit sold at a produce stand in a week in July.

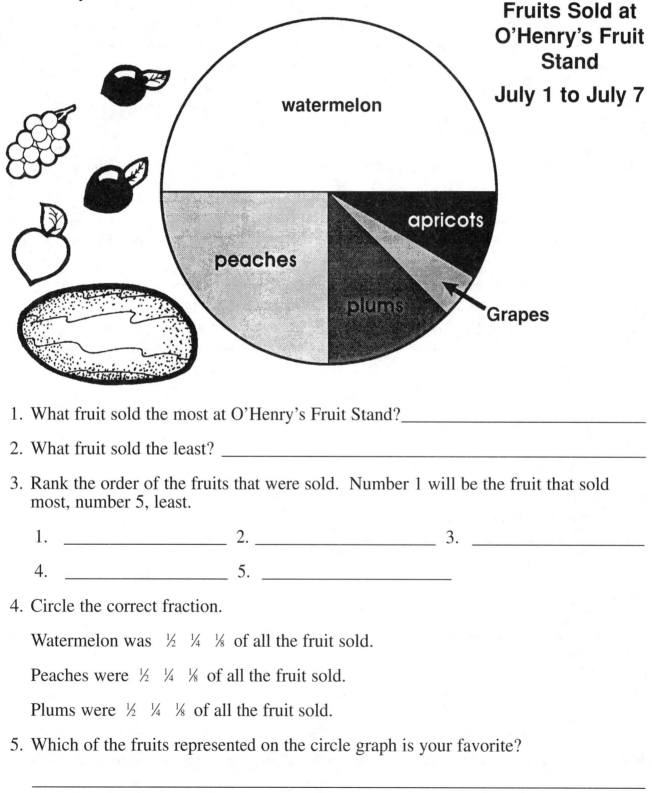

Fruits Sold at O'Henry's Fruit Stand

July 1 to July 7

1. What fruit sold the most at O'Henry's Fruit Stand?_____

2. What fruit sold the least? _____

3. Rank the order of the fruits that were sold. Number 1 will be the fruit that sold most, number 5, least.

   1. _____ 2. _____ 3. _____

   4. _____ 5. _____

4. Circle the correct fraction.

   Watermelon was ½ ¼ ⅛ of all the fruit sold.

   Peaches were ½ ¼ ⅛ of all the fruit sold.

   Plums were ½ ¼ ⅛ of all the fruit sold.

5. Which of the fruits represented on the circle graph is your favorite?

Slices

In a *circle graph*, all the parts must add up to be a *whole*. Think of the parts as pieces that add up to one whole pie.

Look at this circle graph that shows what Chris did during *one hour* of time at home.

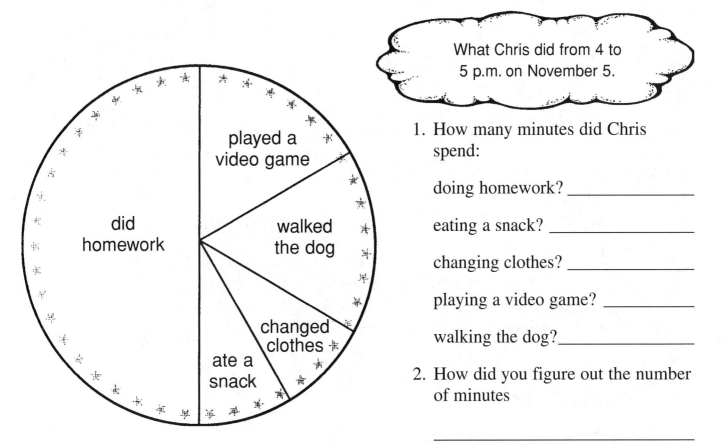

What Chris did from 4 to 5 p.m. on November 5.

1. How many minutes did Chris spend:

   doing homework? _____

   eating a snack? _____

   changing clothes? _____

   playing a video game? _____

   walking the dog? _____

2. How did you figure out the number of minutes

   _____

   _____

Make a circle graph that shows what you did during one of your afterschool hours.

Write the title of your graph here.

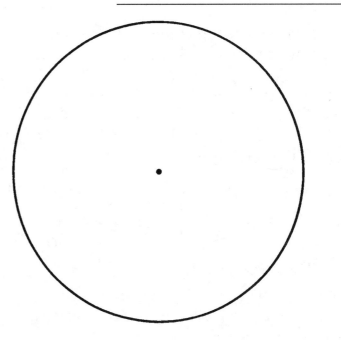

Save the Earth!

At an afterschool meeting of the Applewood Intermediate School Friends of the Earth Club, Mr. Green asked his sixteen club members what they could do to save the earth. They responded at once!

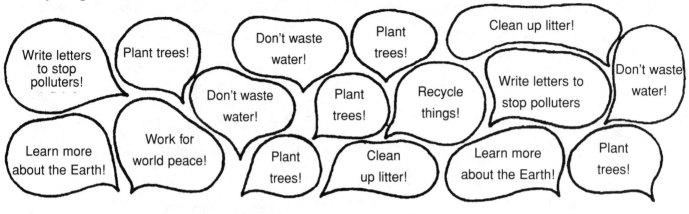

Mr. Green decided to make a circle graph to help the club members see their ideas.

Help him! Use a color key to show the responses. Color each box of the key a different color. Then color in a "slice of the pie" for each response according to the key. Place responses that are the same next to each other, so you will have sections of the same color.

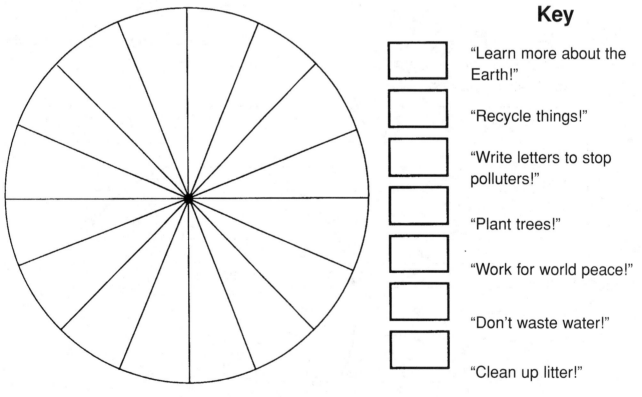

Key

☐ "Learn more about the Earth!"

☐ "Recycle things!"

☐ "Write letters to stop polluters!"

☐ "Plant trees!"

☐ "Work for world peace!"

☐ "Don't waste water!"

☐ "Clean up litter!"

* What could you do to save the Earth? _____

_____

(Use the back of this paper if you need more room.)

Bar Graphs

One type of graph that gives us information is called a bar graph. A bar graph shows us many different types of things by the height or length of the bars.

A single bar graph is one type of bar graph. Questions that ask what kind, what place, how much, how long, and how many can be answered by using a single bar graph.

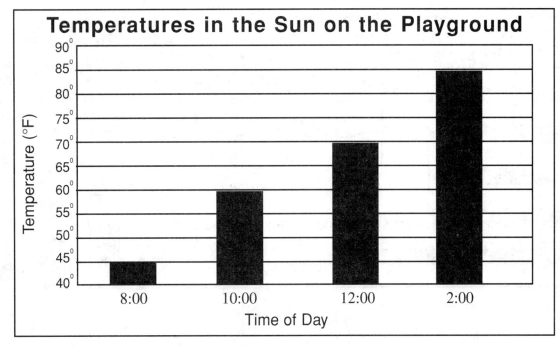

A *double bar graph* (or *multiple bar graph*) is another type of bar graph. It is used to compare two or more things.

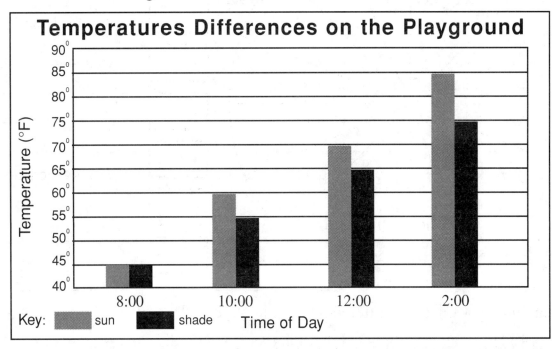

Find examples of single and double bar graphs. Share what you find with your class.

Vertical and Horizontal

The bars on a bar graph may be drawn either vertically or horizontally, depending upon what it is you are graphing. Remember, a graph is a picture, and if you can make a graph suggest what you are measuring, choose the kind of bar that will help "tell the story."

Read these graphs. Then answer the questions below them.

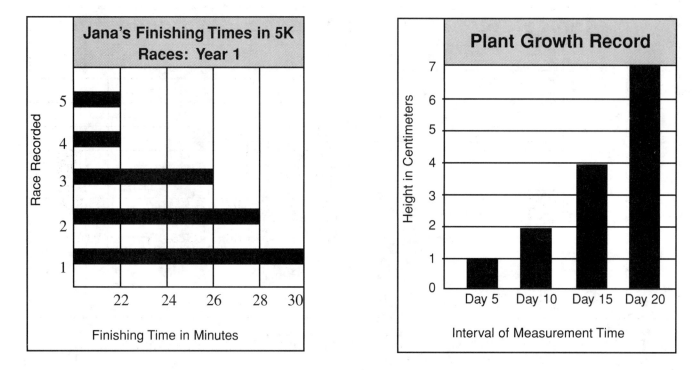

1. Why are horizontal bars used to show race results?_____

    _____

    _____

2. Why are vertical bars used to show plant growth?_____

    _____

    _____

3. What type of bar, vertical or horizontal, would better show the findings on these subjects:

    comparisons of world's tallest buildings?_____

    growth of a snake? _____

    distances baseballs are thrown? _____

    amount of books read by different classes in a month? _____

4. Choose ides from question #3 and graph them as an individual, group, or class activity.

Favorite Subjects

Read this double bar graph that compares the favorite subjects of first graders and fifth graders at Cedar Heights Elementary School.

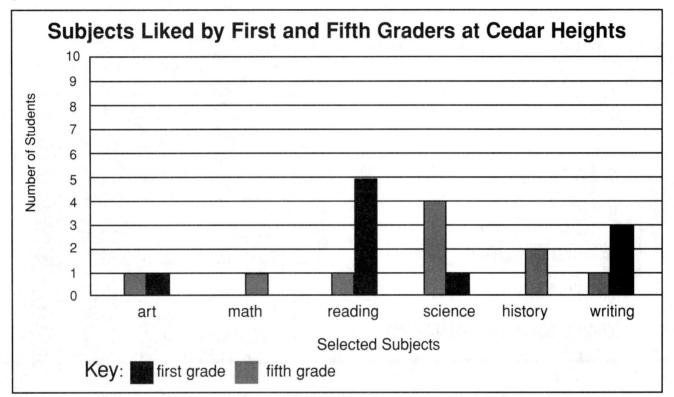

Poll ten first graders and ten fifth graders at your school. Graph the results you find on this bar graph.

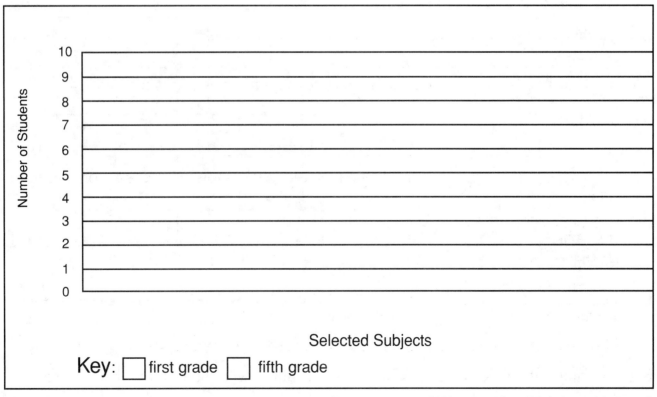

Line Graphs

One type of graph that gives us information is called a line graph. A line graph uses dots and lines to show how things change and compare.

Look at this line graph that shows the average growth for adolescent boys.

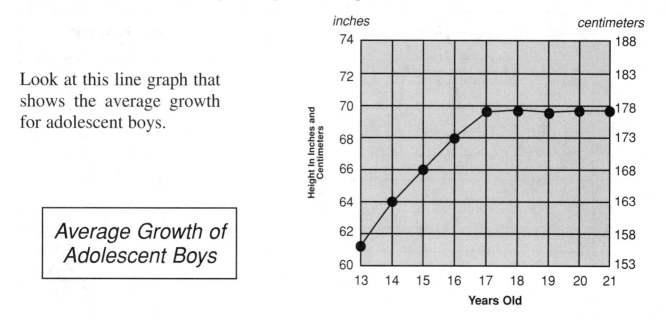

Average Growth of
Adolescent Boys

Sometimes two different things can be compared on the same line graph. A different color or type of line is used for each thing you want to compare. Graphs with more than one color or type of line are called *double line graphs.*

Look at this double line graph that compares the average growth for adolescent boys and girls.

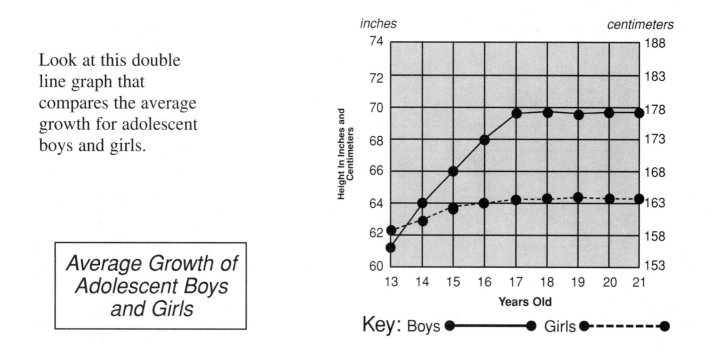

Average Growth of
Adolescent Boys
and Girls

Find examples of single and double line graphs. Share what you find with your class.

Minutes Practiced

Here is a line graph that shows how many minutes a week the Hoopers basketball team practices.

1. On which day do the Hoopers practice the longest? _____

   _____

2. How many minutes does the team practice in a week? _____

   _____

3. How many days does the team practice a week? _____

   _____

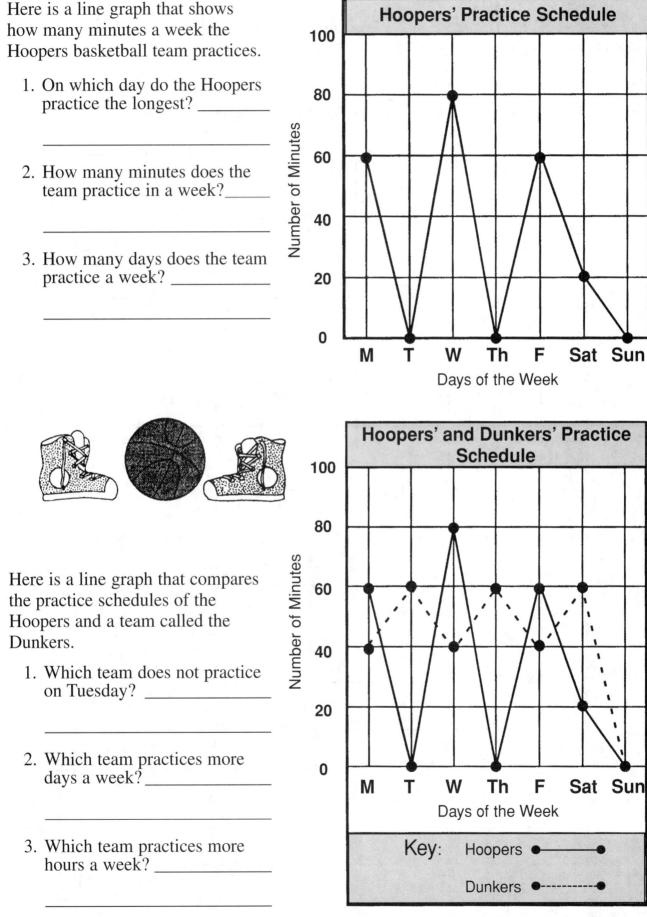

Here is a line graph that compares the practice schedules of the Hoopers and a team called the Dunkers.

1. Which team does not practice on Tuesday? _____

   _____

2. Which team practices more days a week? _____

   _____

3. Which team practices more hours a week? _____

   _____

Hidden Prize!

Jim earned a terrific prize for winning first place in the community talent show. The prize he won is spelled out in this graph.

Find the points on the graph that are identified below. Each point you find will give you a letter of the hidden prize. Can you discover the secret?

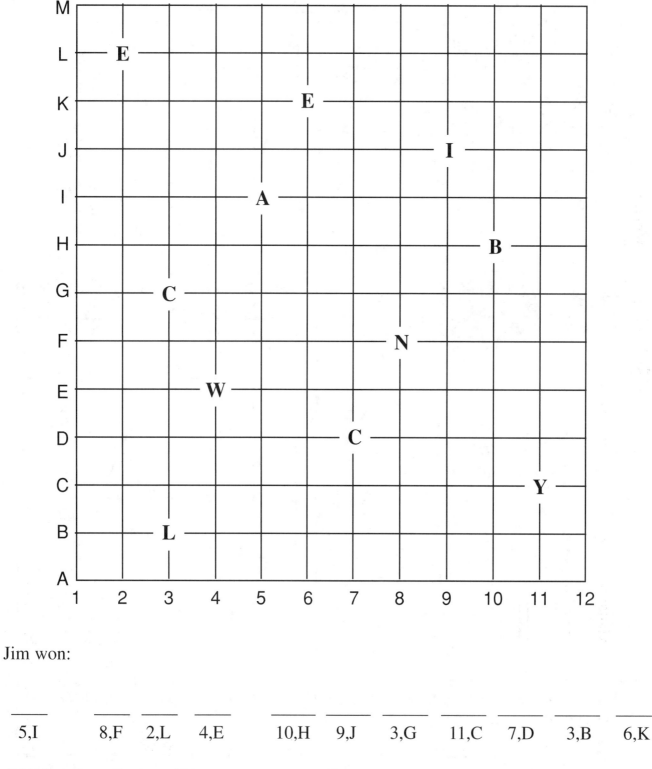

Jim won:

_____   _____   _____   _____   _____   _____   _____   _____   _____   _____   _____

5,I   8,F   2,L   4,E   10,H   9,J   3,G   11,C   7,D   3,B   6,K

Time Lines

A time line is a visual tool that can show events that happen in the order they happen. You read time lines from left to right.

Read this time line of five events in *The Black Stallion* by Walter Farley.

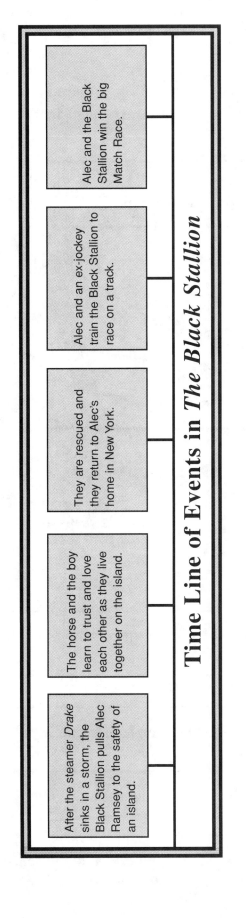

Time Line of Events in *The Black Stallion*

After the steamer *Drake* sinks in a storm, the Black Stallion pulls Alec Ramsey to the safety of an island.	The horse and the boy learn to trust and love each other as they live together on the island.	They are rescued and they return to Alec's home in New York.	Alec and an ex-jockey train the Black Stallion to race on a track.	Alec and the Black Stallion win the big Match Race.

Time lines can be made for events in history. Read this time line of six events in the American Revolutionary War period.

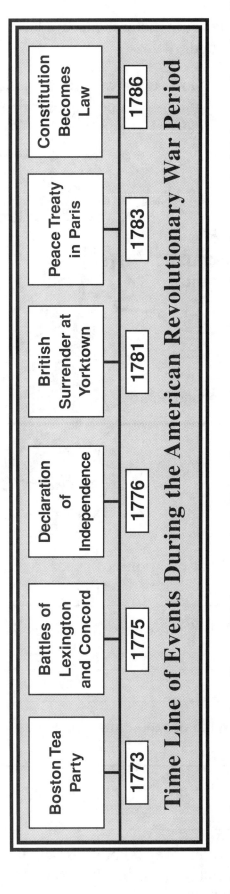

Time Line of Events During the American Revolutionary War Period

Boston Tea Party	Battles of Lexington and Concord	Declaration of Independence	British Surrender at Yorktown	Peace Treaty in Paris	Constitution Becomes Law
1773	1775	1776	1781	1783	1786

Make two of your own time lines. Make one time line of events in a story you have just read. Make another time line of historical events in a time period you are studying.

Diagrams

Diagrams are pictures that are labeled so that a reader can easily learn the parts of what is pictured.

Do you know anything about guitars? Did you know there are different types of guitars? Can you describe the similarities and differences between acoustic and electric guitars?

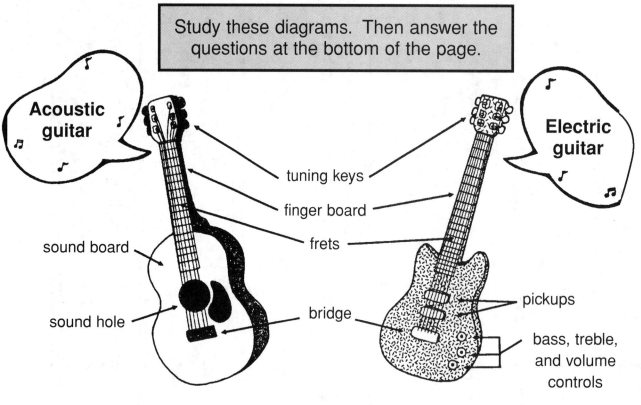

1. What two types of guitars are diagramed? _____

_____

2. What are some of the things these two guitars have in common?

_____

_____

3. What are the things the acoustic guitar has that the electric does not?

_____

4. What are the things the electric guitar has that the acoustic does not?

_____

* As an extension of this activity, research how a sound is made by each guitar. Then, if possible, bring an acoustic and electric guitar to class for demonstration purposes.

Locked or Unlocked?

A diagram gives you information about the parts of something. You can learn where things are, what things do, how things grow, or how things are made by reading a diagram.

This diagram shows the parts of a padlock and how a padlock works.

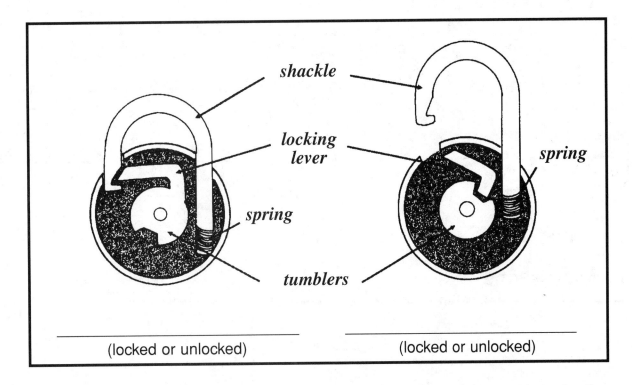

shackle

locking lever

spring

spring

tumblers

_____ (locked or unlocked)

_____ (locked or unlocked)

Two words have been left off the diagram of the padlock: locked and unlocked. Can you label the padlocks correctly by studying the diagram?

Write an explanation of how a padlock is locked or unlocked based on what you have learned by reading this diagram.

_____

_____

_____

_____

_____

_____

*Find examples of diagrams in newspapers and magazines. Make a diagram bulletin board.

Diagram: A Microscope

The following activities will help develop your students' ability to read and make diagrams.

Activity 1: Supply students with diagram "skeletons." (Two are provided for you in this book.) The students may use reference materials to help them complete the diagrams correctly. The teacher may make more "skeletons" to correspond with class curriculum and student interest.

Activity 2: Ask students to make their own diagrams about something of interest to them. Encourage them to share their diagrams with others.

The Parts of a Microscope

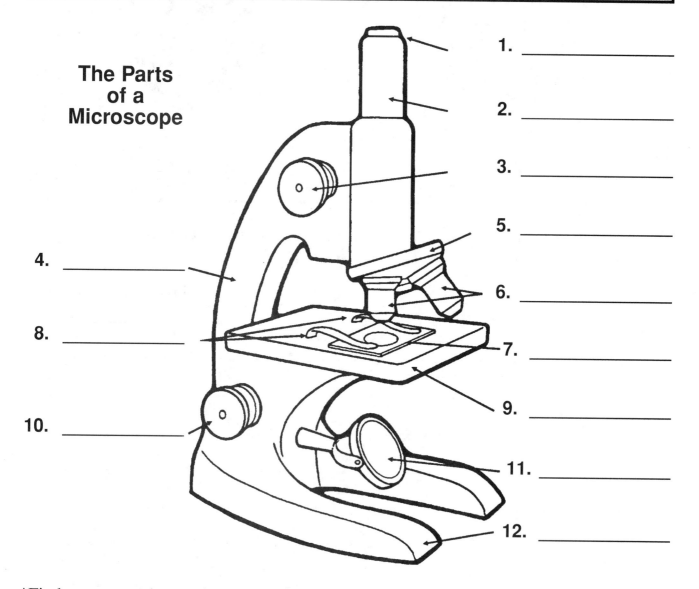

1. _____
2. _____
3. _____
5. _____
6. _____
7. _____
9. _____
11. _____
12. _____
4. _____
8. _____
10. _____

*Find out more about microscopes. Learn how to use one. Share what you know with others.

Diagram: A Fish

Use reference materials to help you correctly label this diagram of a fish.

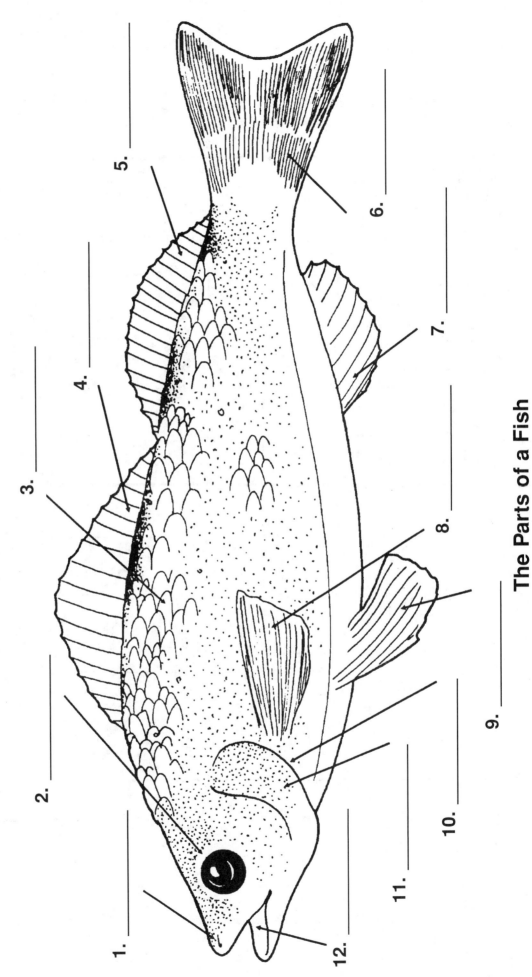

The Parts of a Fish

Ice Cream!

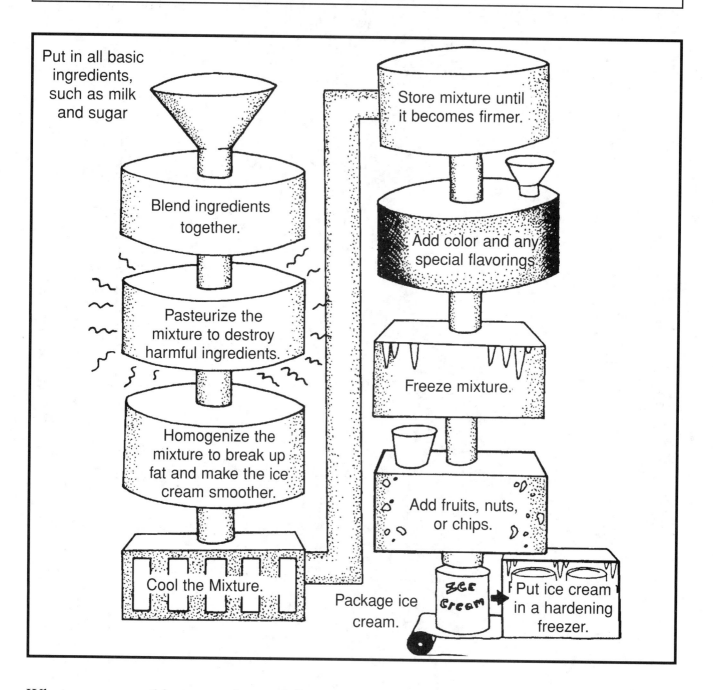

Put in all basic ingredients, such as milk and sugar

Blend ingredients together.

Pasteurize the mixture to destroy harmful ingredients.

Homogenize the mixture to break up fat and make the ice cream smoother.

Cool the Mixture.

Store mixture until it becomes firmer.

Add color and any special flavorings.

Freeze mixture.

Add fruits, nuts, or chips.

Package ice cream.

Ice Cream

Put ice cream in a hardening freezer.

What are some things you learned from reading this diagram about how ice cream is made?

_____

_____

_____

Mind Map

You can make a diagram of you ideas. A diagram of ideas is called a mind **map**.

Look at this mind map of one person's ideas on what to do with afterschool time.

Make a mind map of afterschool activities you would like to do.
Think of at least eight activities

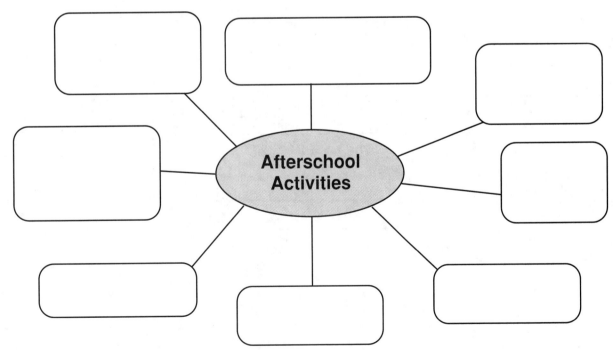

Why and Why Not?

Use this form for mind mapping your ideas on doing or not doing one of the behaviors in the idea box.

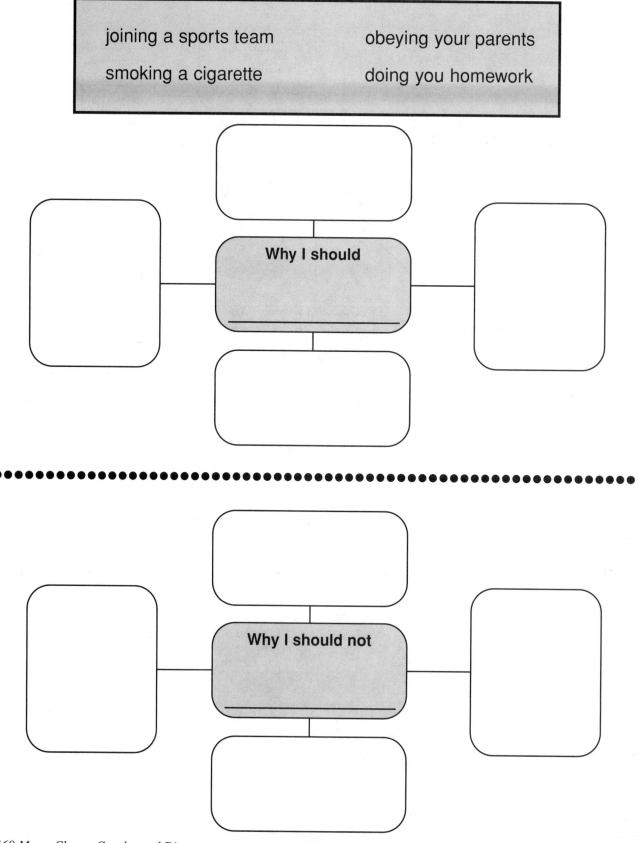

joining a sports team   obeying your parents

smoking a cigarette   doing you homework

Why I should

Why I should not

Form 1

Use this chart form for weekly activities.

Activity	Sun.	Mon.	Tues.	Wed.	Thurs.	Fri.	Sat.
1.							
2.							
3.							
4.							
5.							
6.							
7.							
8.							
9.							
10.							

Form 2

Use this form for a line graph or graph game.

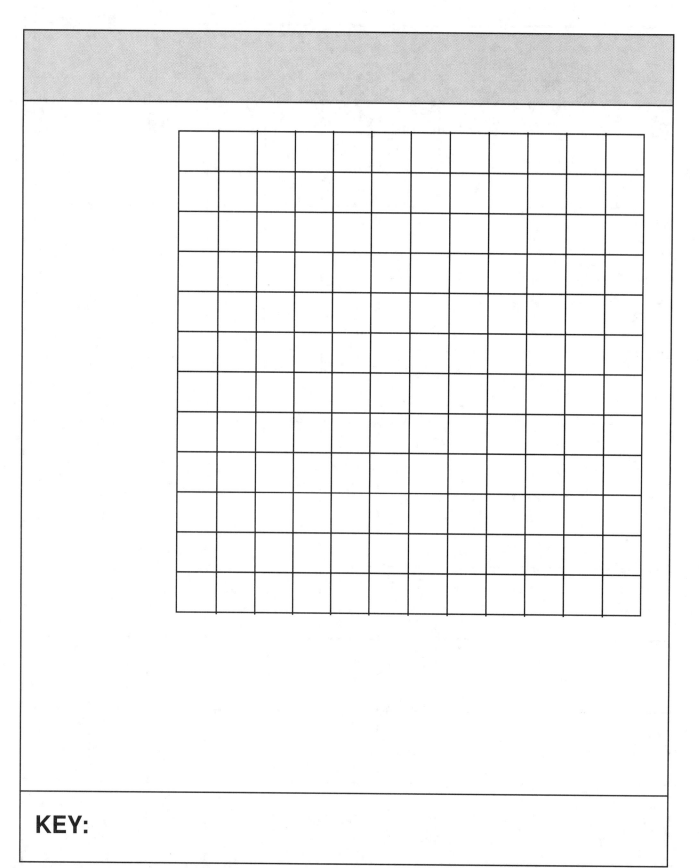

KEY:

Answer Key

Maps, Charts, Graphs, and Diagrams

P. 9

1. southeast
2. west
3. northeast
4. southwest
5. south
6. north
7. east
8. northwest

P. 10

Home=last row, fourth house from the left

P. 11

Several variations are possible. Check as a class activity.

P. 12

Many answers are possible. Here are some ideas.

addition + division + percent %

equals =

stop: sign or signal

no bicycles: bike with line through it

love: heart shape

your country: flag

1. lake
2. school
3. park
4. mountains
5. railroad
6. capital
7. town
8. road
9. airport
10. river
11. forest
12. bridge

P. 13

1. true
2. false; western and southeastern
3. false; northeast
4. false; only one, the others are reached by local roads
5. true
6. true
7. false; west of lake, east of railroad
8. true

P. 15

1. 5 miles (F), 9 kilometers (E), 4 kilometers (C)
2. 2 kilometers (A), 12 kilometers (G), 7 kilometers (E)
3. 3 miles (D), 6 miles (A), 1 mile (F)

P. 16

Answers will vary. Check for appropriate responses as a class discussion activity. Here are some possible ideas.

1.a
2.f
3.c, e
4., d
5.d
6.d
7.b
8.f
9.c, e
10.a

P. 17

1. 20 miles
2. 10 miles
3. 40 miles
4. 20 miles
5. 20 miles
6. 10 miles

It is better from Pleasantown to Mountaintown.

P. 18

1. 1700
2. 550
3. 450
4. 1100
5. 1350
6. 1000
7. 750
8. 550
9. 600
10. 600

P. 22

1. 800 miles
2. about 250 miles
3. 160 kilometers
4. a, b
5. a. Peace River and Grande Prairie
   b. Lethbridge

c. southern
d. 50 miles, 80 kilometers

P. 23

example: silver

A1, white De, gray B4, red D2, ivory C4, silver A2, yellow D1, black C2, purple B3, tan A4, gold C3, brown B1, pink D4, lavender B2, green A3, orange C1, blue

Shaded: A1, A3, B3, C2 Striped: B2, C1, C3 Unmarked: A2, B1

P. 24

1. E2
2. F3
3. C1, D1, E1
4. E5
5. E3
6. A3, A4, B3, B4
7. F1, F2
8. A5, A6
9. D5
10. C4
11. E6
12. B1
13. D4
14. B5
15. C6
16. C2

P. 25

"Products of Argentina" should be colored. Map titles will vary.

1. Indianapolis
2. Terre Haute, Bloomington, Evansville
3. Gary, South Bend
4. Indianapolis
5. Evansville

Answer Key *(cont.)*

P. 26
South America

Africa

P. 27
Answers may vary depending on the source used.

Africa: 11,707,000 sq. mi.
    30,321,100 sq. km

Antarctica; 5, 500,000 sq. mi.
    14,245,000 sq. km

Asia; 17,128,000 sq. mi.
    44, 362,800 sq. km

Australia: 2,966,100 sq. mi.
    7,682,200 sq. km

Europe: 4,057,000 sq. mi.
    10,507,600 sq. km

North America: 9,363,000 sq. mi.
    24,250,200 sq. km

South America: 6,875,000 sq. mi.
    17,806,250 sq. km

Pacific Ocean: 63,800,000 sq. mi.
    63,800,000 sq. mi.

Atlantic Ocean: 31,530,000 sq. mi.

Indian Ocean: 28,356,000 sq. mi.

Arctic Ocean: 3,662,00 sq. mi.

Continents:
1. Asia
2. Africa
3. North America
4. South America
5. Antarctica
6. Europe
7. Australia

Oceans:
1. Pacific
2. Atlantic
3. Indian
4. Arctic

P. 28
1. North America
2. South America
3. Antarctica
4. Europe
5. Africa
6. Asia
7. Australia

P. 29
(Order may vary)

Western Hemisphere
1. North America
2. South America
3. Antarctica

Eastern Hemisphere
4. Africa
5. Europe
6. Asia
7. Australia
8. Antarctica

P. 30
1. Southern, Eastern
2. Northern, Eastern
3. Northern, Western
4. Northern, Western
5. Northern, Eastern
6. Northern, Western
7. Northern, Eastern
8. Northern, Eastern
9. Northern, Western
10. Southern, Western
11. Northern, Eastern
12. Northern, Western
13. Northern, Eastern
14. Southern, Western
15. Southern, Eastern
16. Southern, Eastern

P. 31
1. latitude
2. longitude
3. latitude
4. longitude

P. 32
1. Grand Junction
2. Sterling
3. Denver
4. Lamar
5. Durango
6. Colorado Springs
7. Glenwood Springs
8. Campo
9. Craig
10. Kanorado

P. 35
Check as a class activity.

P. 36
1. south and east
2. Ekalaka
3. Boyes, Hammond, Alzada
4. Boxelder Creek
5. Medicine Rocks

P. 37
1. Far North
2. Southwestern
3. Pacific Coast
4. Plains

P. 38
1. 35 and 40
2. 27
3. Wayne
4. Glen Ridge, 33
5. a. 15
   b. 37
   c. 27
   d. 48

Answer Key *(cont.)*

P. 39
1. a. 31
   b. 45
   c. 37
   d. 88
   e. 51
   f. 85
2. a. 6
   b. 14
   c. 29
   d. 45
   e. 66
   f. 29
3. a. 99
   b. 62
   c. 58
   d. 59
   e. 45
   f. 71

Challenge note: answers will vary, though students should determine that straight, Interstate Highway travel is fastest.

P. 40
1. Sacramento, Oakland, San Francisco, San Jose, Los Angeles, San Diego
2. Needles, Barstow
3. 75 to 100
4. Crescent City, Redding, Bakersfield
5. Answers will vary. Accept logically explained answers, such as desert conditions in Needles and Barstow.

P. 41
1. Brunswick
2. fruit
3. pecans, peanuts, tobacco (other choices are possible)
4. berries
5. corn
6. marble, granite

P. 42
1. Pittsfield
2. Plymouth, New Bedford
3. Boston: 26° to 30°F, –3° to –1°C
   Lowell: 22° to 26°F, –6° to –2°C
   Pittsfield: below 22°F, below –6°C

P. 44
1. a. D3
   b. A1
   c. C3
2. A1, D1
3. State Highway 106
4. B1, B2, C1, C2
5. Mount McGee, Remington, Carlton
6. a. 16
   b. 22
7. Coastline

P. 46
1. 2786 miles
2. 1440 miles
3. 206 miles
4. 2037 miles
5. 802 miles
6. 840 miles
7. 1329 miles
8. 1058 miles
9. 2873 miles
10. 2976 miles
11. 963 miles
12. 417 miles

P. 47
1. April, May, August, September
2. February, June, October
3. March
4. July
5. December 17 at 4:00 p.m.

P. 48
Sunday: Zoo trip
Monday: Soccer practice
Tuesday: Cleaning, library books
Wednesday: Soccer practice, pizza for lunch
Thursday: Bike ride
Friday: History paper due, Mom and Dad's anniversary
Saturday: Grandma here for dinner, Johnny's birthday party

P. 49
1. obsidian
2. sedimentary
3. metamorphic

P. 50
1. 8 pounds, 3.75 kilograms on the Moon10 pounds, 8.5 kilograms on Mars
2. 178 pounds, 81 kilograms on Venus 529 pounds, 240 kilograms on Jupiter
3. 16 pounds, 7.5 kilograms on the Moon 89 pounds, 40.5 kilograms on Venus
4. Jupiter
5. The Moon

P. 51
1. David Peterson
2. $5.80 – Kathryn Ross
3. Barbara Marshall
4. no
5. no
6. 614
7. $48.00

Answer Key *(cont.)*

P. 55
1. 5 pianos, 10 flutes, 30 guitars, 15 drums, 5 trumpets
2. 25, 20, 15, 25
3. Accept any reasonable explanation.

P. 56
1. 1, 150
2. 450
3. 500
4. 550
5. 1,100
6. 300

P. 58
1. watermelon
2. grapes
3. watermelon, peaches, plums, apricots, graphs
4. watermelon 1/2, peaches 1/4, plums 1/8

P. 59
1. homework: 30 minutes; snack: 5 minutes; clothes: 5 minutes; video game: 10 minutes; walking the dog: 10 minutes
2. Answers will vary. Check as a class exercise.

P. 60

Learn 2, Recycle 1, Write 2, Plant 5, Work 1, Don't 3, Clean 2.

P. 62
1. Races are run horizontally, not vertically.
2. Most plants grow vertically rather than horizontally.
3. buildings: vertical; snake: horizontal; baseball: horizontal; height: vertical; books: vertical stacks

P. 63
* Discuss the top graph with the class. Be sure that all of your students can read the graph and are able to make appropriate comparisons between grade levels.
* Encourage the completion of the bottom graph. This would be a great small group activity.

P. 65
1. Wednesday
2. 220 minutes
3. 4 days
1. Hoopers
2. Dunkers
3. Dunkers

P. 66
A new bicycle

P. 68
1. acoustic and electric guitar
2. tuning keys, finger board, frets, bridge
3. sound board, sound hole
4. pickups, base, treble, and volume controls

P. 69
locked (left) unlocked (right)
Explanations will vary. Each explanation must mention the moving of the tumblers to release the locking lever so that the shackle can pop up.

P. 70
1. eyepiece
2. tube
3. coarse adjustment knob
4. body
5. nose piece
6. objectives
7. slide
8. clips
9. stage
10. fine adjustment knob
11. mirror
12. foot

P. 71
1. nostril
2. eye
3. scales
4. spiny dorsal fin
5. soft dorsal fin
6. caudal fin
7. anal fin
8. pectoral fin
9. pelvic fin
10. gill opening
11. gill cover
12. mouth

P. 74
Discuss this mind mapping activity as a class. It should provide for a lively discussion!